THE INDESTRUCTIBLE MAN

The Incredible True Story of the
Legendary Sailor the Japanese Couldn't Kill

DON KEITH AND DAVID ROCCO

STACKPOLE BOOKS

Guilford, Connecticut

Published by Stackpole Books
An imprint of The Rowman & Littlefield Publishing Group, Inc.
4501 Forbes Blvd., Ste. 200
Lanham, MD 20706
www.rowman.com

Distributed by NATIONAL BOOK NETWORK

British Library Cataloguing in Publication Information available

Library of Congress Cataloging-in-Publication Data

Names: Keith, Don, 1947– author. | Rocco, David, 1956– author.
Title: The indestructible man : the incredible true story of the legendary
    sailor the Japanese couldn't kill / Don Keith, and David Rocco.
Other titles: Incredible true story of the legendary sailor the Japanese
    couldn't kill
Description: Guilford, Connecticut : Stackpole Books, [2021] | Includes
    index. | Summary: "Burns, broken bones, shrapnel—nothing could stop
    Dixie Kiefer, the victim of ten wounds in two wars, a veteran of some of
    the U.S. Navy's most celebrated carriers and battles, and a naval
    aviation pioneer"— Provided by publisher.
Identifiers: LCCN 2020046527 (print) | LCCN 2020046528 (ebook) | ISBN
    9780811739641 (cloth) | ISBN 9780811769631 (epub)
Subjects: LCSH: Kiefer, Dixie, 1896–1945. | World War, 1939–1945—Naval
    operations, American. | Yorktown (Aircraft carrier : CV-5) | Ticonderoga
    (Antisubmarine warfare support aircraft carrier) | World War,
    1939–1945—Aerial operations, American. | United States.
    Navy—Officers—Biography. | United States. Navy—Aviation—Biography.
Classification: LCC D773 .K445 2020 (print) | LCC D773 (ebook) | DDC
    940.54/5973092 [B]—dc23
LC record available at https://lccn.loc.gov/2020046527
LC ebook record available at https://lccn.loc.gov/2020046528

♾™ The paper used in this publication meets the minimum requirements of American National Standard for Information Sciences—Permanence of Paper for Printed Library Materials, ANSI/NISO Z39.48-1992.

Contents

From the Authors

A GOOD STORY IS CUT THROUGH WITH COINCIDENCE, IRONY, UNINtended foreshadowing, tie-ins, what-ifs, if-onlys, and almosts. Cut through like sinew that ties muscle to bone to make certain that important work can ultimately get done.

Compelling stories often feature characters that disdain the tried and true. Robert Frost wrote of two diverging roads in a wood, of taking the one less traveled as it bent into the undergrowth. Of wondering where he might have ended up had he chosen the easier way.

A good story contains elements with which anyone can readily identify, but many others can only be experienced when the reader is placed within the context by the teller of the tale.

The best stories are about otherwise ordinary people who find themselves placed in unusual situations and who then do remarkable things.

These are all reasons why Dixie Kiefer's is a truly great tale.

An editor at *Sports Illustrated* once described the work of the late writer Frank Deford thusly: "He'd hang bells throughout the story, and at the end go back and ring every one of them."

We, as the tellers of this tale, can only hope we have done justice to Captain Dixie's story. That we have shown you the what-ifs and if-onlys, connected sinew to bone, revealed to you the destination of at least one man's path less taken, dropped you into the pilot's seat of a hurtling divebomber or onto the heaving, burning deck of an aircraft carrier in the China Sea. That we have been able to help you understand this man and how he was able to do what he did in the face of unfathomable adversity.

We hope that we have hung the bells, and then rung every one of them. Dixie Kiefer deserves no less.

—Don Keith and David Rocco

Interlude

"Captain, you're bleeding pretty bad. Let me get a corpsman up here . . ."

"Naw, I'm okay. They need to be helping the boys down on the flight deck. You see how those five-inch gunners stopped those other three bastards before they could—"

"Captain, your arm, though. Needs to get looked at . . ."

"I'm a tough old bird, Bill. I ever tell you about the time I got run into by a pontoon plane that was buzzing me? At the Canal? Hadda been my head he hit, then the plane would have gone into the drink! Broke my left arm. Now I got a right arm to match. Bring the ship around to one hundred and five degrees. Keep the wind to our starboard so the fire and smoke blows away from the flight deck."

"Here comes a corpsman now, Captain. We got a mattress. Maybe you can lie down here and let him see if he can stop some of that—"

"That last kamikaze was more lucky than good, getting through all the ordnance the gunners were putting up. Keep pumping to the port tanks and maintain our list at ten to twelve degrees so we can keep shoving the burning planes overboard. Keep spilling that burning fuel over the side, too. Tell everybody to look for more suicide planes. They know we're wounded, and if they got 'em, they'll send 'em."

"Jesus, Captain. Looks like you broke both bones in your right forearm. I'm going to wrap it, but you need to go down to sick bay right now and let them splint—"

"Where's the XO?"

"He's . . . uh . . . he's hurt pretty bad. We took him down already . . ."

"I'll stay on the bridge until we have the fires under control."

"Then at least stay still so I . . . sorry, sir . . . I'll try to stop some of this bleeding. How you feeling, sir? You've lost a lot of—"

"How are the men?"

"Uh . . . lots of casualties, sir. But we got a bunch of them that are just as stubborn as their skipper . . . Sorry again, sir . . . staying at their posts, manning hoses, shoving planes and ammo overboard, toting other wounded. They're flat refusing to go to sick bay and get treated. I don't think the navy's going to have enough medals and ribbons."

"Does not surprise me. Every man on this ship is one tough son of a gun. Dixie's kids, I call 'em. Be it typhoon or kamikaze, I've watched what they can do. Ouch!"

"Sorry, sir, compound fracture. Needs to be properly set and splinted—"

"After a while. Hey, Bill, get me updates from the hangar deck and see what damage control says about the fires on the flight deck. Boilers and piping still intact? They've done a fantastic job down there. Let's don't lose it now."

"Aye, sir."

"Be sure they know the bridge is well aware of the job they're doing. We're going to save Big T. She's got a lot more to do in this war, and their captain is not going over the side of another carrier if he can help it. A fellow could get himself hurt doing that."

"We'll tell 'em, sir."

"Fantastic job, men. Now somebody help me up. Let's see how the wind is doing now."

"Captain, steady. You've lost a lot of—"

"Our position looks good, but there's still lots of fire and smoke on the flight deck. Anybody got an update on the hangar deck, just in case we need to try to get some planes in the air? What's the degree of list by now? Casualty update? Any more guns out of commission? Ammo carriers still keeping them supplied, just in case? Anybody heard how Langley is doing? I saw her take a strike just before our first hit. Bring speed to ten knots so the current doesn't keep us floating in that burning oil. Then—"

"*Captain, you're going to have to keep pressure on that wound on your face. It's deep and bleeding like a son of a—*"

"*Will do, but son, I need you to get back down and take care of the boys doing all the work. Tell 'em we got their backs. Show Tokyo Rose the Big T is still in this war. She's indestructible. Long as we have a crew that performs like this. Indestructible!*"

Prologue

Our story begins—as do all stories set on the planet Earth—more than 450 million years ago. That was a time when continents were boldly, brutally shouldering each other around, vying for their own space on an evolving young sphere, rearranging the face of the globe. One particularly violent collision between two such meandering land masses—ones that are now better known as North America and North Africa—created the mountains that would much later be dubbed the Hudson Highlands. These summits are often associated with a hefty, rocky chain that now runs roughly from New England to central Alabama, with other spikes that angle off in varying directions and are labeled with differing names. Some geologists argue that the Hudson Highlands are part of the Appalachian Mountains. Others disagree.

Regardless, long before they were named and branded on maps, and even as the buckling of the earth was still lifting up solid rock and thrusting it thousands of feet into the air, nature began to try to erase the carnage from all this fierce tectonic conflict. The inevitable action of wind and water, freezing and thawing, and then, much later, the boldly charging glaciers that appeared a mere two and a half million years ago, began relentlessly wearing down what appeared to be indestructible peaks. This weather-related erosion continues to this day even as volcanic action deep below the Earth's crust battles back, obstinately shoving upward.

One of the more notable summits in the Hudson Highlands, twin-peaked Mount Beacon, climbs from the east bank of the Hudson River in what is now southern New York State. The north peak is 1,531 feet above the level of the nearby Atlantic Ocean, where the Hudson ultimately empties after flowing on southward and to the west of Manhattan

Island. The other peak to the south, a virtual twin, is just a bit less than a hundred feet taller.

We must note that this scenic location along an ancient spine of violently born, weather-worn mountains is where the story we are about to tell not only begins but also will ultimately and tragically conclude.

Over most of the last five hundred million years, after all the collisions of shifting continental plates, the harsh buckling of ancient rocks, and then the incessant work of wind, rain, rivers, and ice, things remained relatively uneventful around the Mount Beacon area. The first human beings showed up in the region about eleven thousand years ago. By AD 1100, the Iroquois and Algonquians had developed an advanced culture. They considered the twin summits sacred burial grounds and believed that anyone disturbing or disrespecting this place of peaceful eternal rest would be subject to falling under a curse.

Europeans arrived—the French in 1424, followed shortly by the Dutch and the English. It was the English who ultimately dubbed the area New York Colony, named for a duke who would later become King James II (of England) and VII (of Scotland). The area around the shank of the mountain became a center for fabric mills that made use of the wool from sheep raised nearby. Their primary product was socks. The town that sprang up along the eastern riverbank during this period simply continued to bear its Native American name, Matteawan. It would remain so until 1913 when it and a neighboring village, Fishkill Landing, were combined and renamed Beacon, New York.

Then, in the 1760s, there was another shouldering for position by robust and determined forces. That event also created great upheaval and change and altered the face of the planet. This time, though, the shifting was political, not geological.

Colonists, upset with distant and oppressive British rule and what they perceived as indifference to their grievances, boldly rebelled, declaring their independence. They were keen on forming a new country in a new world and were willing to resort to combat if it was necessary to make it so.

The Revolutionary War was on.

With a navigable Hudson River, a newly manned fort at West Point just to the south, and with General George Washington, the leader of the rebel Continental Army, setting up headquarters directly across the river from Mount Beacon in the town of Newburgh, Matteawan and environs became a strategic location for the bloody rebellion. If the British meant to divide and conquer the revolting colonies—separating the firebrands of New England from the more moderate settlers to the west—the Hudson Valley would be the obvious place to hammer in that wedge.

The British followed traditional military tactics, moving slowly and predictably. Well aware of this fact, Washington directed that signal-fire positions be established on the mountaintops. Some would be elaborate, intricately planned and constructed, while others were quick and makeshift. The men stationed up there could observe troop movements from those heights or be informed by spies with details of what was about to happen. When such intelligence came, the fires were to be lit to signal Washington and his army or the garrison at West Point.

Optimistically, standing orders were in place for another use of the beacons. The signal fires would be lit and fireworks shot off atop the mountain to celebrate the inevitable victory over the Redcoats and the establishment of the new and free government of the United States of America.

In 1778, the new state of New York adopted its seal, coat of arms, and flag. They each feature a scene with two ships on the Hudson River, a sailing sloop and a masted schooner. In the background is Mount Beacon.

Beacon would boast other notable events and citizens over the coming years. One of the better-known natives would become an important figure in yet another bitter upheaval, World War II, which more than a century and a half later would yet again disrupt the planet and redraw the atlases. James V. Forrestal, the son of Irish immigrants, was born in what is now Beacon in February 1892. He went on to become secretary of the navy during the war and later our country's first secretary of defense, each position under President Franklin D. Roosevelt. The navy's first super aircraft carrier, the USS *Forrestal* (CV-59), would one day be named for him.

At this point, we will also mention that Secretary Forrestal will play a small but key role in our story. That includes providing a quote that supplied the title for this book. Also playing a role will be other examples of those remarkable warfare-changing vessels—aircraft carriers. Be assured, though, that their participation in the tale will be significantly more pronounced than Forrestal's.

In 1900, the Daughters of the American Revolution (DAR) erected a monument atop Mount Beacon to honor the Revolutionary War patriots who manned the signal fires. Two years later, the Mount Beacon Incline Railway was completed at a cost of $100,000, allowing visitors to much more easily make their way up the steep slope from the river valley to the mountaintop, to the ancient burial ground of the Native Americans and the locations of the beacon pyres. The funicular would eventually be abandoned in 1978 and then later destroyed by an arsonist's blaze in 1983. Efforts have been made by a nonprofit volunteer organization, the Mount Beacon Incline Railway Restoration Society, to resurrect it, but so far the incline railway has not been rebuilt.

The mountain attracted numerous visitors who believed the clean air—often 10 degrees cooler than in the valley along the river—and mountain springs were therapeutic. For many years, a casino attracted customers from all over the area, including those who came upriver from New York City, sixty miles to the south. The establishment featured live bands and dancing as well as wagering. Notorious bank robber Willie Sutton was a regular there, and locals claimed that John Dillinger and Bonnie and Clyde also visited at least once.

The popular movie star Robert Montgomery was also born near Mount Beacon, in 1904, in the town of Fishkill, just north of the mountain. The actor served as a commissioned officer in the US Navy during World War II. He was aboard a destroyer that took part in the D-Day invasion in June 1944.

Beginning in 1909, famed film director D. W. Griffith made three short films near the DAR monument on Mount Beacon. One of them, *The Redman's View*, tells a story about the cruel treatment of Indians by white settlers, spinning the account in only fourteen minutes. While the film features the beauty of the area, it is not at all an accurate portrayal of its history.

It was 1928 when the first towers for the new medium of radio broadcasting sprouted on the north peak. It was so early in the development of the technology that no one realized elevation and rocky soil were not necessarily good for stations transmitting on the wavelengths then employed. The first broadcasters had trouble with their signals reaching their intended listeners and soon moved transmitters and towers to lower ground, more conducive to propagation. Just after World War II, the towers of FM stations, which employ a wavelength at which elevation extends the range of the signals, would once again appear there.

Renowned folk singer and social and antiwar activist Pete Seeger lived in a log cabin on Mount Beacon and was energetic in preserving the history and natural state of the region right up until his death in 2014. He protested war, racism, and the destruction of the environment well into his nineties.

With the coming of the aviation age, the twin peaks that climbed so steeply into the sky from the Hudson quickly took on an ominous nickname. Newspaper accounts of the airplane crashes that occurred there spoke of "The Aerial Graveyard." Despite a series of bright beacon lights on the radio towers along the ridge, the mountain's steep slopes, the area's sometimes brutal weather, and the sudden increase in the number of aircraft in the sky meant that the otherwise placid ridge would sometimes get in the way of aircraft.

Such a victim was a US Navy Curtiss SBC "Hell Diver," a biplane with two men on board. The two-seater roared into the fog-shrouded northeastern flank of Mount Beacon on the rainy, windy night of September 14, 1935, killing both fliers. They struck the ridge at a 45-degree angle and almost certainly died instantly.

Dancers at the nearby casino heard the crash. Other observers at the bottom of the mountain reported hearing the plane's engine and saw its running lights disappear into the murk. Even so, because of the rain, fog, and wind, the wreckage was not located until the next morning. Civilian Conservation Corps volunteers from nearby Putnam County went to great lengths to bring the bodies of Lieutenant Lincoln Denton and Aviation Machinist Mate Clinton Hart across the top of Mount Beacon to the Incline Railway. From there, the bodies of Denton and Hart were carried to waiting ambulances. The Mount Beacon Fire Tower ranger acted as the communication contact point for the recovery operation. The casino was designated as the staging area for the recovery operation. Sadly, a number of local vandals destroyed and swiped a great deal of the wreckage for souvenirs, including an aerial machine gun. Most of the rest of the debris was shallowly buried in the hard, rocky soil on the mountain ridge.

The pilot of the doomed plane, Lincoln Denton, was a commercial artist who had joined the US Naval Reserves primarily to indulge his love of flying. Being prepared to serve his country if needed was a side benefit. Denton was a fine arts graduate of Harvard University and a native of Houghton, Michigan. His flight—and death on Mount Beacon—came on the final day of the two weeks of full-time service he gave to his country each year. He was twenty-seven years old and unmarried.

The other victim of the crash, Clinton Hart, was Denton's mechanic. A native of Brooklyn, New York, he was twenty-eight years old and lived in Brooklyn, just off Flatbush Avenue, with his wife. That was within walking distance of Floyd Bennett Field, where their ill-fated flight originated. His ashes would be interred at Arlington National Cemetery.

The two aviators, accompanied on the entire training run by another "Hell Diver," had flown a circular route together from the airfield in Brooklyn, where the reservists were based, to Detroit, Michigan. They were almost home, on the last leg of the trip, after taking on fuel at Albany, New York. But then, south of Mount Beacon and Peekskill, Denton inexplicably turned away and circled his biplane to the northeast, passing over the city of Peekskill. We will never know why. The pilot of the other aircraft radioed Denton to come back around and continue following him. The young lieutenant did not respond.

Denton and Hart soon flew into bad weather. The other plane and its two occupants continued south, experiencing good flying conditions, and made it safely back to Floyd Bennett Field.

The portion of the mountain where Denton and Hart died was then known by some locals as Schofield's Ridge. Today it is better known as Fishkill Ridge.

This catastrophic event serves as powerful but ominous foreshadowing for how our story will eventually play out just over ten years later.

But first, we must go two thousand miles west and thirty-nine years back in time—to Blackfoot, Idaho, and 1896—for the birth of one Dixie Kiefer, a man who would prove almost indestructible.

Almost, though, can be such an unforgiving word.

CHAPTER ONE

A Boy Named Dixie

WHO KNOWS WHAT CONSTITUTES A HERO IN THE MAKING? WHAT traits are inborn and which ones are learned and practiced? Why do some ordinary men and women rise above fear and pain and, when faced with seemingly overwhelming circumstances, do remarkable things? And inspire those around them to also do more?

What factors cause certain people to be natural leaders of men, universally respected and admired? Is it hereditary? Learned?

On a different note, why is it that so many men and women who eventually serve their country aboard an oceangoing warship are born and raised so very far from salt water?

We know of nothing that marked Dixie Kiefer for eventual heroism and leadership when he was born on April 4, 1896. His place of birth was in landlocked Blackfoot, Bingham County, Idaho, a burg located just south of the Snake River but a long, long way from salt water. The area averages just eleven inches of rain per year.

Regardless, Kiefer would grow up to become a participant in and hero of historic naval battles. They would be fought in faraway and much wetter and more dangerous places than Blackfoot, Idaho. Locations like the Coral Sea, Midway Island, and the China Sea.

Dixie came into this troubled world only about a decade after the area in southeastern Idaho had seen its first permanent white settlers but more than eleven thousand years after the first humans inhabited the region. His birthday was less than twenty years after President Ulysses Grant declared nearby Yellowstone the world's first national park. Exactly two

Commodore Dixie Kiefer, summer 1945, his right arm still in a cast from injuries suffered while serving as captain of USS *Ticonderoga*.

years before the start of the Spanish-American War. And only a couple of years after a "ditch" was dug from the nearby river to irrigate Blackfoot's streets and grow trees of such uncommon height and beauty that sightseeing parties came from all over the region to view them.

It is also interesting to note that Dixie was born at the same time that governments in faraway Europe were negotiating and signing treaties that were aligning nations into two distinct and opposing camps. Russia, France, and Great Britain came together in an agreement that would come to be known as the Triple Entente. Meanwhile, the new German emperor, Kaiser Wilhelm II, pointedly dissolved his successor's alliances and, determined to pass England as the world's greatest naval power, began building capital ships at an unprecedented rate. Even in the mid-1890s, as Dixie Kiefer was born to Tina and Carl in Idaho,

Europe was preparing for the next great war. One that would give Dixie his first taste of battle.

As of this writing, neither Blackfoot's official website nor its Wikipedia page mentions the birth of the infant Kiefer in their town. There apparently is no monument to him there, no memorial that would indicate this baby born in their municipality would grow up to one day command a mighty ship and accomplish heroic and amazing things on behalf of his nation and its allies.

The area's dry climate is favorable for one thing: The town of Blackfoot has long been known as "The Potato Capital of the World." This fact, in addition to the nearby location of the East Idaho Fair and the view of the stunning sunset behind the distant Tetons, is what is emphasized by the town boosters.

Maybe they simply are not aware. It was only a few years after the boy's birth in their town—and also that of his younger sister, Idanha, in 1903—that his family made what was just another in a series of moves. The 1900 census found them in Spokane, Washington. Later, they headed farther west, briefly out to California, much closer to the sea.

Both of Dixie Kiefer's parents were first-generation Americans, children of German immigrants. His father, Karl Edward Wilhelm Kiefer—who over the years employed a variety of variations of his given name, including "Edward C.," "Carl," "Karl," "H. G.," and even "E. C. W."—was born in Allegheny County, Pennsylvania. For simplicity, we will call him "Carl."

Both of Carl's parents, Dixie's paternal grandparents, died long before the boy was born out there in potato country. They would never know how the youngster turned out or the extraordinary things he would eventually do.

Carl Kiefer grew up to become an insurance agent and to dabble in real estate, first in the Pittsburgh area where his family had settled. Later, he made a move west to Denver, Colorado. Records from the era show that he represented protection through a variety of different insurance companies. It was in Colorado that he met and married a young lady named Maggie, a union that did not last long or produce children. Their divorce would get Carl Kiefer's name into the legal annals of the state when Maggie sued him for an increase in alimony after the final decree. She also accused him of living in adultery with his second wife, a Nebraska girl named Christina Glade. Christina was Dixie's mother.

The whole thing was a complicated dispute in which Maggie questioned whether the divorce was final in Colorado before Carl married Christina over in Nebraska. The eventual decision by the judge—in Carl's favor—did set enough of a precedent to become part of case law in the state. Attorneys and judges still reference the case today.

The Nebraska girl whom Carl married, Christina Glade, was also a first-generation citizen of the United States. Hers was another German family that came to America seeking opportunity ahead of what would prove in the 1900s to be a difficult time for their native nation. The Glades overcame true hardship in their new country but eventually found notable success.

Christina's father (Dixie's grandfather), Henry Glade, had been born in Hanover in 1844, the youngest of twelve children. He was only four years old when his parents emigrated to America on a sailing vessel. It took them thirteen weeks to make the voyage to New Orleans. They soon continued their move, going on up the Mississippi River to St. Louis. It could have been they were trying to get as far from salt water as they could after that trying passage. It was more likely, though, that they were simply following so many other Germans who had found a home in St. Louis.

Unfortunately, both of Henry's parents died soon after getting to St. Louis. Siblings and other displaced Germans raised Henry Glade, at least until he decided he was old enough and struck out on his own. He found himself in Iowa and, though still not yet a teenager, learned through on-the-job experience the flour milling trade. By the time he was fourteen years old, he was in charge of a mill all on his own, supervising men twice and three times his age, showing remarkable leadership for someone so young.

We might safely assume that Dixie Kiefer inherited his determination, self-reliance, and leadership skills—ones that made him such a fine military man—from his grandfather Henry, as well as the bravery and resilience to carry on regardless of hardship.

The young Henry Glade wasted no time in putting to use the things he had learned in the mills where he worked. He soon constructed his own flour mill, hired and oversaw a crew there, and then scouted around and bought another, this one in Grand Island, Nebraska. Along the way, he also met and married Catherine Etting, the sister of a business partner. Together, Henry and Catherine raised five children, four boys and a girl.

That lone girl, of course, was Christina, Dixie's mother. She was born in March 1870. Each of the boys would one day help to run their father's highly successful milling businesses. Christina would meet and marry a recent divorcé from Colorado named Carl Kiefer and immediately begin hopscotching around the country.

One of Christina's brothers, Fred Glade—Dixie Kiefer's uncle—happened to be a talented athlete and walked away from the family business for a bit to take an interesting side trip. He became a professional baseball player in the major leagues, eventually a starting pitcher for the St. Louis Browns and the New York Highlanders (a team that later became the Yankees). He was the first pitcher in major league history to toss a shutout and then hit a home run for the game's only score to win it, one to nothing. After his baseball career—finishing with a lifetime earned-run average of 2.62 and 107 complete games tossed—Fred came back home to Nebraska and rejoined his brothers in the milling business, leaving the baseball diamond behind.

There Fred met and married a pretty, young Christian Scientist from Missouri. Her name was Dixie Husband. The new Mrs. Fred Glade, then, became the namesake for her sister-in-law's third child, a boy, and the primary subject of our story. Christina had a penchant for naming her children after members of her family, maybe as an antidote for all the time she spent away from them after marrying Carl. The Kiefers' first child, born in Wisconsin in 1892, was named Henry Glade Kiefer, after Christina's father. Next came Catherine, born in Colorado and named for Christina's mother. Then there was Dixie and Idanha, out there in

Idaho. We now know about Dixie's given name, but we cannot be sure where Idanha got her most unusual one. It may well have come from an ornate new hotel completed and opened in Boise only a few years before her birth in the same state. The inspiration for Carl's and Christina's last girl cannot be confirmed, but one note says that Phyllis Glade—called "Honey" by friends and family—may have been named for Christina's brother, Filbert. She arrived in this world in California, where Carl and Christina and their brood had by then temporarily landed.

Both Kiefer boys, Henry and Dixie, eventually served their country in the military, and Catherine married a major in the US Army Air Corps. Henry was a first sergeant in the Signal Corps during the final months of World War I. Dixie would receive in 1915 an appointment from Nebraska's 1st Congressional District to the US Naval Academy in Annapolis, Maryland, and would continuously serve for more than thirty years, including seeing battle action in two world wars.

None of the Kiefers or Glades—including young Dixie—could have ever guessed where that war-shortened Naval Academy education would eventually take him, what he would do in the service of his country, or how he would one day contribute so mightily to helping defeat a fanatical enemy.

Dixie's time at Annapolis would be reduced by the critical need for naval officers, experienced or not, in what was then known as the Great War. Not yet "World War I," because no one could have known for certain that there would ever be a World War II. The Great War was, after all, often referred to as "The War to End All Wars." Many truly believed that optimistic prediction.

Nor could anybody have known that Dixie, the kid born and raised so far from any ocean, would stretch that career at sea—and in the air above it—long enough to fight in and survive both worldwide conflicts.

Carl and Christina Kiefer divorced not long after the birth of their youngest daughter, Phyllis. We have no record of what caused the split, but we can guess it may have had something to do with Carl's wandering and Christina's desire to be near home and family back in the Midwest. Carl remained in California (the Fresno area), met and married his third wife, Charlotte Burch, and had two girls, half sisters to the rest of the Kiefer clan. For that marriage, Carl officially used the name Edward C. Kiefer.

Christina—or "Tina," as Dixie always called her in the many beneficiary forms, requests for reimbursement, and other naval paperwork he filled out over the years—promptly returned with her children to the Midwest after the separation. She never remarried, even though she lived a long life. She would not pass away until September 1949, at the age of seventy-nine, a long time in which she and Phyllis often resided with Dixie, crisscrossing the country and even the Pacific Ocean, following him to whichever home port it was from which the United States required her son to sail.

Unlike their father—who divorced twice and married three times in an era and place in which even one dissolution of nuptials was unusual—neither Dixie nor Phyllis ever married.

It is another curious aside to our story that Carl Kiefer, a man who employed so many different given names in his time, fathered a son to whom he and his wife awarded only a single moniker.

Dixie Kiefer had no middle name. "Dixie Kiefer" was all there was.

This ironic oddity would perplex Academy professors, navy yeomen, military record-keepers, citation authors, genealogists, and other sticklers for accuracy from the very beginning to the tragic end of Dixie Kiefer's long and stellar career.

Chapter Two

War and Peace and War

THE FIRST OF THE SIX YOUNG MEN ASSIGNED TO ASSASSINATE ARCHduke Franz Ferdinand simply lost his nerve. There was a policeman standing behind him, too close. The boy was afraid he would be caught before he could hurl the bomb he carried at the heir apparent to the Austro-Hungarian throne. He did not even try. He simply stood and watched as the intended victim passed only feet from him, hoping the policeman did not see his knees shaking or the bulge of the bomb he carried in his jacket.

The second would-be assassin, the next down the motorcade route, boldly pulled out his device and gave it a mighty heave. However, he was so exuberant that the bomb skidded well past its target and exploded beneath the fourth car in line, not the second one. Not the vehicle in which Franz Ferdinand and his wife rode. The driver of the archduke's open convertible had been half expecting such an attack all along. He instinctively punched the accelerator and sped away. That made it impossible for the other four assassins to make any kind of attempt to mortally correct perceived political wrongs.

It was June 1914, and the European continent was a hot cauldron, already boiling, threatening to spill over into war.

Later that same day, Archduke Ferdinand ignored the advice given him and headed out to visit those injured in the earlier botched attempt on his life. He felt it critical that he not show fear of those who disagreed with him enough to murder him. He even asked his wife, Duchess Sophie Chotek, to go along with him, riding next to him in the open car.

However, on the way to the hospital, his driver took a wrong turn. When he realized his mistake, the driver jumped on the brake and grabbed the gearshift, trying to reverse his route before someone could shoot or heave another bomb. In the process, he stalled the car's engine. As he cranked away, trying to get the vehicle restarted, a young man near the curb with dark hair and a thin mustache watched, not believing his sudden good luck.

Gavrilo Princip, one of the original six assigned killers, now stood only a short distance away from his quarry, the young would-be assassin still upset about his earlier failure. But now, here was his intended victim, stopped cold right in front of him, not five feet away. Princip did not hesitate. He quickly pulled his pistol from his belt and fired two shots, fatally wounding Archduke Ferdinand. One of the bullets also struck the duchess, gravely wounding her. She would soon die, too.

That errant turn on a Sunday morning in June 1914 in Sarajevo, Bosnia, would soon redirect the fates and lives of millions of people around the world. Few of them recognized or understood the significance of the assassination. Practically no one in the United States understood the convoluted history and politics that would soon so greatly alter their own future.

That included Dixie Kiefer, a stocky young man who had just completed an unremarkable junior year at Lincoln High School in Nebraska. A young man who loved roughhousing, playing football—even though he got banged up doing so—and his mother's cooking.

The assassination of the archduke and duchess was the flint spark that ignited the war in Europe. That smoldering fire would quickly flare into the Great War. The first declaration of war came on July 28, 1914. Within a week, Russia, Belgium, France, Great Britain, and Serbia were aligned against Austria-Hungary and Germany. The shifting alliances that had started about the time of Dixie Kiefer's birth had finally led to war. The United States was slow to the party. They would not enter the fray until April 1917, in part driven by public outrage when a submarine, a German U-boat, sank the British passenger liner *Lusitania* the previous year. Few wanted to get involved in a war that seemed so far away, so complicated.

By the time America did enter the world war, Dixie Kiefer had completed high school and was already a second-year midshipman at the

US Naval Academy. We have no evidence that the conflict in Europe or the likelihood of the United States joining in was the impetus for Dixie seeking an Academy appointment. It is just as likely that he saw this as an opportunity to get a good education and graduate as a naval officer. Even though he would complete only three years of the typical four required for a service academy degree, he, like most of his classmates, was awarded his diploma and his commission as an ensign. He was ordered to active duty in the US Navy on May 31, 1918. The navy needed officers.

Like his brother's, Dixie's wartime service was short. Peace came officially on November 11, 1918, a day formally declared Armistice Day. *Armistice* means "truce" or "a temporary end to hostilities." That proved to be an accurate definition in the case of this particular world war. Few of those gathered in Paris to sign the Treaty of Versailles were interested in anything temporary. The costs of this conflict were breathtakingly high.

Once again, the map of Europe would necessarily be redrawn. That would soon lead to more bickering and seething resentment. But even more chilling, the war had cost the lives of nine million soldiers and sailors and ten million civilians. Almost 120,000 of those were Americans. Twenty-one million people were wounded. During World War I, the term *newfangled* came to mean "able to kill people and destroy things." Innovations like tanks, fixed-wing aircraft, submarines, railway guns, automatic weapons, flame-throwers, and poison gas had done their work well. Less destructive inventions had also been utilized, with the telephone and wireless communications employed for the first time in battle.

The victorious allies had convinced themselves that if this was truly going to be the war that prevented all future wars, the treaty would have to create a post-conflict world that would guarantee there would be no more such horrible conflicts. Humans had simply become too effective at killing each other. Those who lost the war were to be severely punished, effectively emasculated; they would be saddled with such substantial reparations that they would never again be able to create such a deadly war machine. The victors would also make it less likely that any other nation, seeing the potential for what would happen to them should they fail, would dare ignite such a wide conflagration.

The sanctions did not serve either purpose. What those harsh treaty terms actually did was throw Germany's economy into a deep depression. People were starving. Factories were shuttered. The poor were even poorer and the rich lost fortunes overnight. Those who managed to keep some of their money found it virtually worthless. Inflation was so out of control that Germans burned money for heat in winter because it was cheaper than firewood.

The harsh terms of the Armistice actually kindled an unexpected fire. A proud people had been humbled. At first, Germans saw no way out, nor any leader who could return their nation to some semblance of its former glory and prosperity. Then, at exactly the right time, a charismatic but fascist leader would emerge. The treaty had inadvertently created a vacuum that eventually gave rise to a regime that promised to correct the wrongs of the brutal reparations. As a result, another world war would come, one with an even wider reach and capability for awful destruction, suffering, and death. It included an alliance with a sacred emperor from the other side of the planet.

Dixie Kiefer was certainly aware of what was going on in Europe even as far back as high school in Lincoln. The war was likely foremost in his mind by the time he accepted the appointment from his representative in Congress and reported to Annapolis, scheduled to graduate as part of the Academy's class of 1919. He could not know whether the war would still be raging when he finished the Academy and received his commission—a commission that would put him in a position to lead other men to battle all the way across a broad ocean.

Then, when the United States entered the fray in 1917, Kiefer was no longer preparing for a peacetime naval career.

"Oh, look at the crowd over there!"
"Crowd—hell! That's not a crowd, that's Dixie Kiefer."

That was how the 1919 edition of *The Lucky Bag*, the Naval Academy's yearbook, started the biography of portly Midshipman First Class Dixie Kiefer. He was clearly popular with his classmates.

"Good-natured, impulsive, generous, he makes friends everywhere, and when he gets the ordeal of reporting aboard a ship over with, he will make a good officer and, in an emergency, mighty fine ballast," the yearbook continues, poking friendly fun at Dixie's girth.

That description would apply to Kiefer for his entire career. One sailor who served under his command would one day declare, "I will give one million dollars cash to anyone who can truthfully say anything bad about Captain Kiefer!"

He may have become a sailor's skipper, but back then he was hardly a lady's man. *The Lucky Bag* also talks about "how he hid behind the piano in Rec Hall the day a fair inhabitant of our modern Athens came to see him." But then, "After two years spent here without even looking on at a hop [dance], Dixie suddenly succumbed and began taking dancing lessons, and now he rivals Vernon Castle [a well-known dancer of the time on Broadway and in silent movies]."

On the last day of May 1918, Kiefer received orders to report to the USS *St. Louis*, a troop transport ship that had previously been the ocean liner SS *St. Louis*. He had to be pleased he was shipping out on a vessel named after his grandfather Glade's former hometown. The ship was berthed in New York City. Dixie was commissioned a regular ensign a week later and was sworn in while crossing the Atlantic on the *St. Louis*, steaming toward France.

Assigned to the Destroyer Force and based in the port of Brest, in the province of Brittany in the far northwestern reaches of France, Kiefer's first duty as a fledging naval officer was on a most unusual vessel. The USS *Corona* (SP-813) was actually a yacht outfitted as a patrol craft, protecting shipping from U-boats in the North Sea. It was hazardous duty in an inhospitable body of water, made even more treacherous by the notorious German subs. The job required constant observation and then dodging torpedoes already in the water, headed their way.

Dixie survived that duty as well as his first world war, but an even more dangerous assignment awaited once the peace treaty was signed.

He continued to be based in Brest after the war ended, alternating shore duty at naval headquarters with service aboard the salvage and wrecking ship USS *Favorite* (SP-1385). Then he moved to the USS *Chesapeake* (ID-3395), a vessel whose primary job was clearing leftover armed, live German mines still deployed in the North Sea. So far as we know, he saw no battle action, but his time on both of those ships offered tough, workmanlike duty and no little danger. Kiefer survived that peril as well. It was a good learning experience for him.

From all indications, he did a good job and showed promise as an officer. Along the way, he was promoted to the rank of lieutenant (junior grade).

It was almost a year and a half later—in October 1919, about a year after the end of the war—that he finally was detached and sent back to New York. He had precious little time to visit with his mother, brother, and sisters. Next up was his assignment to the USS *Pennsylvania* (BB-38), a relatively new battleship that had not participated in the war.

She had been berthed at her home port in Yorktown, Virginia, when the United States entered World War I. Though available and capable, she spent the entire war on the US side of the Atlantic primarily because she was ahead of her time. Unlike most other battleships of the day, *Pennsylvania* was powered by fuel oil, not coal. There was simply not enough oil available in Europe to supply such a gas guzzler. If she was that far away, operating in the areas where the sea war was the most intense, it would not be practical to send the required amount of fuel to her. She was not invited to the dance. She would, however, get plenty of chances to show her stuff later on.

Kiefer reported aboard *Pennsylvania* on New Year's Day 1920, just in time to ship out for maneuvers in the warm Caribbean. In April, he had the opportunity to meet and shake the hand of the president of the United States, Warren G. Harding, who came aboard for a reception.

At first glance, it might appear that Dixie Kiefer had found a home on this ship in particular, and on battleships in general. All indications are that he enjoyed the duty and that he did an admirable job. However, even though he served aboard the big vessel for almost two and a half years, until May 1922, the young officer was already considering his future, both in and out of the navy.

As a warship, *Pennsylvania* certainly would have a better future than she did a past. She continued to serve her country until February 1948. That included being heavily damaged by the Japanese at Pearl Harbor, Hawaii, on December 7, 1941, being repaired and put back in service six months later, and participating in her share of action for five years in World War II. She was later used as a target in nuclear bomb tests at Bikini Atoll in the South Pacific in 1946 and was finally given a funeral at sea, deliberately sunk.

During his more than two years aboard the battleship, Dixie had been thinking hard about what he really wanted to do in the navy, assuming he decided to go ahead and make it his life's career. And he had pretty much decided to do just that, as he very much liked being in the navy. He had also been doing some serious talking with his fellow officers, as well as his skipper on the *Pennsylvania*, Captain E. H. Campbell.

Unlike many in the navy, Kiefer was no longer convinced that the future of naval warfare lay in bigger and badder battleships. The race to produce the most frightening dreadnoughts had consumed many of the world's navies, requiring huge chunks of their military construction budgets.

Like Kiefer, though, some were convinced that a new kind of sea war would be fought in the future. With the advent of better and more dependable aircraft and the development of ships on which they could land and take off, the way sea battles would be fought, should there ever be another war, was about to change dramatically. With an aircraft carrier loaded with small, nimble—but deadly—planes, a navy no longer had to rely totally on land-based airfields. Soon they could literally drive the airfield to wherever in the world it was most needed, so long as there was a sizable patch of ocean available in which to park it.

Yes, Dixie knew he could remain on battleships and likely one day captain his own ship. Battleships, despite their cost, were not going away, and certainly not before his career ended. And he was more than confident enough in his ability to someday successfully command such a ship.

But now, with considerable seagoing experience under his belt, it was time to explore what Kiefer saw as a far better option. It was one in which he could best serve his country if his suspicions about the future of naval warfare were correct.

Oh, and he could have a hell of a good time along the way, too.

His decision would one day place him in the middle of the first sea battle in which neither fleet would ever see the other, a clash in which the fighting would be conducted almost entirely by carrier-based aircraft. That showdown would be dubbed the Battle of the Coral Sea.

On April 6, 1922, while his ship was in the Navy Yard at Bremerton, Washington, for refitting, Dixie Kiefer typed up a memo on USS *Pennsylvania* stationery, signed it, and submitted it to Captain Campbell.

> SUBJECT: *Request for aviation duty*
> *Reference:*
> *(a) Bunav Manual Part C, Chapter 1, Section 2.*
> *(b) Bunav Radio 6029–1710.*
>
> 1. *It is requested that I be ordered to duty with the next class for instruction and training in aviation to begin 1 July 1922.*
> 2. *I have completed four years sea duty subsequent to graduation from the Naval Academy.*
> 3. *If this request is granted it is requested that I be allowed to proceed by land paying my own expenses with thirty days delay.*
> 4. *I have had no leave during the fiscal year.*

The request came as no surprise to his skipper. Captain Campbell approved the request the very next day, subject to Kiefer reporting to the Navy Board of Medical Examiners "for preliminary physical examination for aviation duty."

That one condition gave Dixie pause. His last couple of annual fitness reports had pointedly noted that he was putting on weight and should attempt to lose a few pounds. The grub on the wardroom table was tasty and plentiful, and, as *The Lucky Bag* had good-naturedly noted, he had long struggled with his weight. Could that issue now possibly get in the way of his exciting new journey?

The physical exam took place the same day as Campbell's tentative approval, so there was no possibility of a crash diet in order to prepare for the scales. Dixie need not have worried. The doctor's report was a single sentence: "Examined this date and found physically qualified for aviation duty."

Then, the next day, Captain Campbell sent a note to everyone who mattered: the chief of the Bureau of Navigation, the commander of Battleship Division Seven, the commander of Battleship Squadron Four, and the commander in chief of the US Pacific Fleet. He gave a glowing recommendation, noting, "Lieutenant Kiefer is an excellent officer, energetic, capable, cool and self-confident. I consider that he has the temperamental qualities required for aviation duty."

So it was that Kiefer was on his way to the white sand beaches of Pensacola, Florida, to learn how to fly "heavier-than[-air] aircraft, involving actual flying in aircraft, including dirigibles, balloons and airplanes." His skipper's description also foretold just how Dixie would later perform in some of the most stressful and trying circumstances anyone could imagine.

Dixie Kiefer had just made a fateful decision, one that would one day place him on the bridge as second in command of an aircraft carrier. He would play a major role at two of the most unique, intense, and momentum-changing sea battles of the next world war, the one nobody thought would ever come. It was also a career shift that would eventually put him at the helm of another carrier where his cool leadership, self-confidence, capability, bravery, and skills would save the vessel and many of its crewmembers from almost certain destruction and death.

Meanwhile, in Germany, a young man with a hypnotic ability to influence a crowd when he spoke had the previous year begun holding a series of raucous rallies, mostly in beer halls. Adolf Hitler had already been voted chairman of a relatively new political party, the National Socialist German Workers' Party, by a vote of 533–1. No one knew what to make of this firebrand, but most believed he was too radical and wild-eyed to ever be a threat, either to his own people or to the world.

On the other side of the planet, the leader of what was at the time the world's third-largest naval power, Japan, had just agreed to sign the Washington Naval Treaty. This was a promise to bring home Japanese soldiers who were occupying a portion of Siberia and to agree to leave the Pacific Rim as it was, with no further hostilities or territory grabs.

The rest of the world relaxed, enjoying the building financial boom and rising feelings of postwar optimism.

The Roaring Twenties were just getting going.

Dixie Kiefer reported for flight instruction on June 30, 1922. When he arrived at Naval Air Station Pensacola as a "Student Naval Aviator (Seaplane)," the young lieutenant only knew that his career was suddenly looking up. Up into a bright blue sky that formed a canopy above the emerald-green waters of the Gulf of Mexico.

And he was also certain that his mother and sister—Tina and Honey—would love it there.

Dixie Kiefer early in his navy career.

Chapter Three

Learning and Leading

We do not know whether Dixie Kiefer's aim from the beginning was to command an aircraft carrier. The United States was just getting serious about these amazing vessels while he was at the Academy. We do know that most of his next two decades in the navy were dedicated to flying planes or running carriers: learning how to fly, teaching others how to fly, inspecting airplanes under construction for the navy, and testing their capabilities as they were launched, usually by catapult, off carriers. And then serving as an officer aboard several of those big flat tops.

Fresh out of school at Pensacola, Kiefer was ordered to join VO Squadron Two aboard USS *California* (BB-44), not a carrier but a battleship, based in San Diego. "V" is a designator meaning "heavier than air," and "O" indicates that this was a "marine observation" unit. The big warship was equipped with catapults from which airplanes could be launched to fly around the area and radio back what they could see from up there. Early versions of the aircraft, before radio was robust and reliable enough, used carrier pigeons to send messages back to the ship. Many battleships still carried cages and birds, even after radio had effectively replaced them.

Being fired off the catapult on the ship's deck—very much like a slingshot—was hazardous enough, but using the plane's pontoons to land on the water and get into position to be retrieved by the vessel was infinitely more difficult and dangerous. Several veterans of such flying—the way aircraft was necessarily utilized before the first flat-deck carriers were put into service—have proclaimed the operation "the toughest, roughest, most dangerous flying in the aviation world."

Newly minted naval aviator Dixie Kiefer was already pushing the boundaries.

The aircraft they used were small seaplanes, equipped with pontoons. Once their observation mission was completed, they were required to land at near-stall speed on the wave tops while approaching a sled being towed by the battleship. Then, without hesitation, the pilot had to crank his engine back up to maximum power in order to run up onto the "recovery" sled. Next, he had to cut power at the precise second in order to engage a sling connector. Finally, a crane on the ship's deck would lift the aircraft and its pilot back up onto the catapult, ready to be fueled and hurled off again when needed. All these tasks had to be accomplished regardless of the wind direction and speed or the sea state at the time.

Piloting such planes was Kiefer's first job as a naval aviator in San Diego. He was accompanied on the flights by a radioman but no carrier pigeons. When he had the chance, from the ship on which he learned to carry out all of these risky maneuvers, or from his Vought UO-1 aircraft, he could watch as other pilots practiced landing on a big platform on the nearby beach. It had been constructed at the edge of the water to simulate a carrier approach. This was a beginning, but the platform was stationary, always in the same spot, facing the same direction all the time. Eventually, the navy needed a real flat top on which to practice.

The USS *Langley* (CV-1), the first US aircraft carrier, would be based there soon, becoming part of the Pacific Battle Fleet in November 1924. That finally gave the carrier-pilots-in-training the chance to perform real takeoffs and landings from a vessel built specifically for the purpose.

Aircraft had been flown off ships for several years already, and there were even some flat-deck carriers in use during World War I. However, it was during the interwar period that the development of this new type of naval vessel shifted into high gear. Others in addition to Dixie Kiefer had seen the advantages of having a strong carrier fleet, ready to deploy wherever needed.

The *Langley* had served as a collier—a ship that carried coal to the fleet—during World War I. Afterward, a big flight deck was constructed on top of her main deck, running most of the length of the ship. A series of major events in naval aviation history soon followed.

In October 1922, the first US Navy pilot flew an airplane off a moving ship. This was also the first time a plane relied mostly on its own power to get airborne from a vessel's flight deck. Nine days later, another pilot became the first to land an airplane on a flat-deck carrier while it was under way.

On the night of November 11, 1924, a day by then officially designated as Armistice Day, and just two days before *Langley* officially became part of the Pacific Fleet based in San Diego, Dixie Kiefer added his own "first" to the growing list of aircraft carrier "firsts." That evening, as the *California* sat anchored in San Diego Harbor, Kiefer climbed into his Vought airplane and cranked up the engine.

The UO-1 was first designed as a seaplane but later added the ability to convert to a wheeled aircraft for ground and carrier landings. It was a two-seater, intended to carry a radioman in addition to—and seated directly behind—the pilot. It carried about eighty gallons of fuel and had a range of almost four hundred miles. And it could cruise at more than 120 miles per hour.

Sitting there in mostly darkness that night, Dixie Kiefer gave a thumbs-up to the ship's bridge. Instantly, the vessel's big searchlights were turned on, trained on a spot in the harbor about a thousand feet ahead. Then, after another signal, Dixie revved his engine as the catapult tossed the one-ton airplane skyward. Just as it had done so many times before. So many times before, perhaps, but always in sunny daylight.

Dixie Kiefer had just become the first man in history to "fly" an airplane off the deck of a battleship—or any ship, for that matter—at night. Compared to all the other accomplishments and firsts when it comes to naval aviation, that takeoff may not seem like much. However, to those for whom it mattered, it was a truly historic event. The accomplishment still pops up in aviation history books.

We know from his service records that Kiefer had become an excellent flier, even if he was still getting those notes about his weight whenever he took the required flight-physical examinations. We also know he was doing well at his job because his next move was back across the country to Pensacola in December 1925—this time to be an instructor, to show others how it was done.

A Vought UO-1 aircraft being catapulted off a battleship in San Diego Harbor. Dixie Kiefer became the first man to pilot a plane, similar to this one, off a ship at night.

The navy was well aware that in order to take advantage of the new carriers coming on line, they would need an abundance of well-trained flyboys. The USS *Lexington* (CV-2) and USS *Saratoga* (CV-3), both of which had started construction as battle cruisers, had the plans changed mid-build and were instead completed as carriers. This was another indication that the US Navy was anticipating the future of sea warfare.

Lexington was launched only a month before Dixie Kiefer made his move back to Florida to teach. She was placed into service about two years later, in 1927. *Saratoga* was on a very similar timeline. More and bigger aircraft carriers were on the drawing board or in various stages of construction. The *Lexington*-class vessels could carry between seventy-eight and ninety airplanes. Each one required a pilot. Supplying this need for competent fliers would be Dixie's job for the next year and a half. The navy would one day have an urgent need for each and every one of his students.

One of those pupils was a young man from Danville, Illinois, named Joe Taylor. Like many others who were learning to become navy pilots under Dixie Kiefer, Taylor and his mentor would cross paths

A Vought UO-1 aircraft being recovered by a destroyer.

many times over the next two decades, including aboard a carrier in the throes of battle. Taylor would eventually receive three Navy Crosses for his heroics in the air.

During this time, Kiefer received one of the few black marks on his service record. That is, besides all of those admonitions about his weight, one of which scolded him for being forty-four pounds heavier than the navy wanted him to be. Even this particular negative incident turned out to be a minor paperwork snafu, coming as the result of a very brave and helpful mission in which the lieutenant took part.

In the spring of 1927, areas along the Mississippi River in Arkansas, Mississippi, and Louisiana suffered what has been called the most destructive flooding in the nation's history. An estimated five hundred people died and more than seven hundred thousand were left homeless.

At the height of the disaster, Kiefer took a group of pilots and other personnel from the Pensacola Naval Air Station and flew over to assist in any way they could. Their first task was to fly over the affected area, marking flooding on maps so officials could determine just where help was most needed. Kiefer also advised the state and federal rescue agencies on the best ways to use aviation in search, rescue, and replenishment efforts.

On a low-altitude flyover one afternoon, Dixie noticed below him a barn surrounded by floodwaters. There was a group of people clinging to the roof, trying to escape the rising waters. From their desperate arm-waving, he knew they were in serious trouble. Even though there were tall trees surrounding the building, Kiefer flew in low to see for himself how bad the situation was. Depending on how long they had been there atop the barn, they could be suffering from exposure, dehydration, and hunger, and the rushing river could sweep them away if it continued to rise.

Then, to the dismay of the radio operator in the rear seat, Dixie suddenly reached over and cut off the plane's engine.

He glided in just a few feet above the stranded survivors; then he dipped his wing on that side of the aircraft as he sailed past them, stuck his head out the window, and shouted, "I'm sending help! Stay strong!"

Then he restarted his engine—which fortunately kicked right in—before he could lose any more altitude. He flew away to report the plight of those trapped people. They were rescued by boat before dark, their lives probably saved by Kiefer's sharp eye and unusual maneuver.

Kiefer and his men did more than fly, though. They also assisted with shovels and other tools, helped pile sandbags, and did other dirty work when called upon.

Kiefer later received letters of praise and thanks—copies of which were placed in his personnel file—from Major Malcolm Elliott, the US Army Corps of Engineers commander of the Louisiana Rescue Fleet, and from John E. Martineau, the governor of the state of Arkansas. The major wrote, "You not only performed all tasks assigned to you with energy and resourcefulness but were exceptionally diligent in seeking out opportunities to be of service." Governor Martineau offered a detailed thank-you, writing, "You responded to the call of your country in this great crisis with promptness and dispatch, assisting us in our task of rescuing marooned people on levees and house tops, saving thousands of lives, superintending the strengthening of levees day and night in order to avoid further catastrophes, erecting refugee camps, giving first aid, transporting food and clothing, distributing and administering typhoid and smallpox vaccine to prevent epidemic, and similar work for the relief, comfort and health of our flood sufferers."

The black mark on his record? The bean counters back in Pensacola sent Dixie Kiefer cash to be used by the men on temporary duty as a per diem for food and other incidentals. Kiefer, obviously busy saving lives, did not respond quickly enough with an accounting of how much money he had given each man under his supervision. Dixie took care of it when he could and the issue blew over, but it is still a part of his permanent record.

Then, in late June 1927, Kiefer requested yet another move—a big one. He wanted to go back to Annapolis, the Naval Academy, for a whole new tack. Kiefer had decided he wanted to study aeronautical engineering.

Again, we can only assume his motivation. A giddy optimism had seized the country during the 1920s. The stock market was booming. Technology was racing to keep up with the demand of a thriving economy. War was the furthest thing from the minds of most US citizens, even as the military took advantage of prosperity to add new hardware.

It is quite possible that Dixie, with the world at peace, was by this time thinking about life after the service. He had been able to care for his mother and sister on his officer's pay. But what would civilian life offer? His experience in flying and teaching others to become pilots would likely serve him well in the aircraft industry. Factories were buzzing to meet the needs of commercial airlines as well as the military. The US government had subsidized air-mail systems in the mid-1920s, and there was already demand for passenger airlines. As the economy continued to grow at a torrid pace, more people would naturally want to get across the country quicker. Should there be another war—unlikely as that seemed during the Roaring Twenties—Kiefer knew that aircraft, including those flying off carriers, would be a key asset. Whether he was still in the navy or out in the civilian world, someone who was expert at those flying machines would be in demand.

Besides, Dixie loved airplanes and flying them. He knew he wanted to make his career in some aspect of aviation once he left the service. He opted for the technical side.

This time using US Naval Air Station–Pensacola stationery, he completed his request for a change of duty. And again, he must have discussed it beforehand with the commandant at Pensacola, Captain Frank B. Upham, as well as with the Naval Academy, because the approval came quickly, only one week later.

"I request that I be considered an applicant for the Post-graduate Course in Aeronautical Engineering starting the summer of 1936," he wrote. "I am a graduate of the Naval Academy Class of 1919, entered aviation training in June 1922, and qualified as a Naval Aviator in March 1923. Since that time I have been doing actual aviation duty in active squadrons of the Battle Fleet, except for the past nine months when I have been employed as a flying instructor at this station."

Captain Upham's approval consisted of two sentences: "Approval recommended. Lieutenant Kiefer is an excellent pilot and an asset to the aviation organization."

So Dixie went back to school, successfully completing the demanding course in June 1929, receiving his master of science degree. He actually completed some of his coursework his last year at Massachusetts Institute of Technology in Cambridge.

Then, for the following few months, Dixie Kiefer was busy jumping from one assignment to another at places like the Naval Aircraft Factory in Philadelphia; the Pratt and Whitney airplane plant in Hartford, Connecticut; the Wright Aeronautical Corporation in Paterson, New Jersey; and the Bureau of Standards in Washington, DC. Most of his duty was working with navy inspectors, observing the work of the various companies under contract to build aircraft for use on those new carriers. It was also a learning exercise so Kiefer would be even more of an expert on such planes, inside and out. He soaked it all in. What he learned would one day stand him in good stead.

On the same set of orders that sent him off to all the plant observation duty, the US Navy's Bureau of Navigation (BuNav) completed his instructions by telling Kiefer he would be going back to duty aboard a ship, an aircraft carrier. We still do not know whether he knew he was destined to be on carriers for the balance of his naval career, but, with a single line on a long list of orders, the die was cast. He was to report to the CV2: "On 20 September 1929, you will regard yourself detached; will proceed and report to the commanding officer of the U.S.S. *Lexington* for duty involving flying with VS Squadron 3B, Aircraft Squadrons, Battle Fleet."

After several weeks of leave, he was to report aboard the *Lexington* in the midst of a most ill-starred period of time, late October 1929. The stock market was already having seasick gyrations, prices soaring and plunging like a heavy sea. Then, less than a week after Kiefer showed up at his new duty station in San Diego, all the built-up ecstasy and unrestrained confidence of the Roaring Twenties disappeared over a two-day span with a $30 billion drop in stock market valuation.

The Great Depression was under way and would last for most of the next ten years. And that two-day crash would also play a role in what Dixie Kiefer would be doing over the next fifteen years of his life.

Kiefer likely would not have looked upon the coincidence of his new job with the economic crash as a bad omen for him personally. It was simply time for him to report for his next assignment, doing what he enjoyed doing, while serving his country. He would once again be flying observation aircraft but in a squadron, one that also had a few fighter planes, too. Dixie's mother and sister moved to San Diego and shared housing with him there, just as they had done whenever possible with all of his previous meanderings.

The Depression had little effect on the Kiefers and their daily lives.

Not so for people in other parts of the world. The economic collapse in the United States was just part of a global breakdown. Germany, for example, was especially hard hit, and at a time when progress was finally being made to get past the calamitous times after the Great War. Millions lost their jobs. The country's largest banks collapsed. Aristocrat and common worker alike shared the misery. Few escaped the effects. This was precisely the opening Adolf Hitler and his fascist party needed to gain the support of the German people. A suffering populace listened attentively as Hitler stood before fervent rallies, ranting against the party in power. And many of them responded to his promises to lead the country back from Depression, renounce the Treaty of Versailles, restore the country to its former glory, rebuild the economy, and put people back to work.

Japan, too, was hit hard by the worldwide economic crash. The island nation had a different problem than Germany, though. The country had few natural resources. Almost everything had to be imported, including steel, iron, oil, rubber, bauxite, and other materials necessary to fuel its industrial demands. That included equipping the military as the country grew more and more aggressive, attempting to build its defenses by offensive means against any potential conqueror, real or imagined. But with a worldwide depression, the Japanese had no way to market the goods it did produce domestically. Customers were broke. Japan could no longer depend on exports to pay for the natural resources it had to purchase abroad. The emperor and his military leaders were convinced that the only way to grow strong, to ensure their sovereignty, to build defenses, and to get the raw materials the nation needed was to seize territory where those things were available. Only then could they grow a mighty empire that could defend itself and become a major international power. Only with that power could the Home Islands remain safe and independent. Politicians or citizens who objected to such belligerent logic were shoved aside, and the Japanese went looking for nations to master.

Anyone in the military would have had to know that those storm clouds on the horizon might eventually mean another worldwide war. Dixie Kiefer would have known that his own training and that of the men he oversaw was in preparation for bloody conflict. Even so, there was a strong feeling of isolationism in the United States. Many felt overcoming the Depression and putting people back to work was the top priority, not getting caught up in yet another distant war among countries most Americans would have had trouble locating on a map.

Thankfully, though, men like Kiefer continued to get ready for the unthinkable, and others kept developing war machines as they could, just in case they were ever needed again, either on the battlefield or to act as a deterrent to those who would dare start such a conflagration. Such costly construction was a hard sell, but at least it provided jobs for people who now desperately needed them.

In January 1934, while Dixie was commanding officer of VP Squadron 4-F, Aircraft Squadrons, Pearl Harbor, he had his first close encounter with a potentially deadly fire. But not his last.

By all indications, Dixie enjoyed his job heading up the squadron. He had a number of his former student pilots from Pensacola in the group, too. That included Joe Taylor, one of the guys Kiefer had already marked as a potential asset should there ever be a shooting conflict that required them to face real action as opposed to the endless drills and exercises.

One day the Fleet Air Base's twenty-four-foot motor/sail craft was tied up at the finger pier next to squadron headquarters while taking on fuel. Suddenly there was smoke everywhere. Somehow a fire had broken out in the boat's bilges.

Dixie Kiefer saw what was happening from his office window. He did not hesitate. He rushed outside and took charge of the situation, directing those nearby to shut off the fuel pump and retrieve the CO_2 fire extinguishers that were stationed all around the pier.

But he did not just stand back and give orders. He joined the fight.

In his eventual commendation, E. W. Tod, commander of Aircraft Squadrons and Attending Craft, Fleet Air Base, praised Kiefer for "personally direct[ing] fire extinguishers into the burning bilges and, at considerable hazard to yourself, continu[ing] to fight the fire which was by that time under the poop deck of the motor sailer and almost inaccessible. Your prompt action, presence of mind, and persistence at great personal risk in fighting this fire undoubtedly prevented greater damage to this motor sailer."

As noted, this is the first instance for which we have a record of Kiefer having to dive in and fight a blaze. It prophesied, though, a much more serious situation in which he would one day find himself. He would handle it much the same as he did this one, but the commendation for that act of bravery would be more than a simple memo in his official record.

Dixie jumped from one assignment to another during the 1930s, serving on USS *Saratoga*, going back on shore duty at Pearl Harbor, getting promoted to the rank of lieutenant commander, doing more shore duty in Hawaii and San Diego, becoming engineer officer, and again being promoted, in 1939, this time to commander.

It was early in this period, in March 1931, while serving aboard *Saratoga*, that one of Dixie Kiefer's beloved flying machines reached out and bit him in one of the most unusual aircraft accidents ever. At the time, his ship, the aircraft carrier *Saratoga*, was conducting exercises near the US Submarine Base at Coco Solo, on the Atlantic Ocean side of the Canal Zone, Panama.

One day while Kiefer was standing on the ship's deck, one of his fellow Vought O2U seaplane pilots buzzed him, getting much closer than the flyboy intended. Dixie instinctively threw up his left arm when he realized the plane was zooming past so close. Before he could even duck, though, the plane's pontoon struck him as it flew by.

Kiefer could not believe it! He had been hit by an airplane in flight and would live to tell about it. But then the pain started and he realized he had been seriously injured.

The blow broke his left arm in three places. *Saratoga* crewmembers rushed him to the submarine base dispensary for emergency treatment. The next day, he was transferred to Gorgas Hospital in the Canal Zone. There the doctors recommended that because of the seriousness of the break, he should be treated at the hospital and not be allowed to leave with his ship. Kiefer explained that it was not his first serious bone fracture: He had broken his left ankle and split his kneecap playing football as a kid back in Nebraska, and had healed up just fine from those injuries. But the navy docs insisted.

Saratoga, her job finished in the Canal Zone, steamed away without him. After six weeks in Gorgas Hospital, Dixie appeared before a medical examining board. They considered his X-rays and decided he needed still more treatment at a stateside navy hospital. It would be almost a full year later—May 1932—before the US Navy conducted a special flight physical examination at Pearl Harbor and certified that he was once again fit to fly aircraft solo. The paperwork did advise that he be kept under observation by the squadron's medical officer. And the memo ended by suggesting that Kiefer "institute measures to reduce his weight."

A naval board of inquiry found Dixie Kiefer blameless in the unusual incident. The investigation determined that he "was in no way responsible for the accident" and that "the injuries received by Lieutenant Kiefer were incurred not as the result of his own misconduct." We have no report of whether the other pilot suffered any punishment for flying his plane into Kiefer. Dixie carried the scars proudly and would often tell the story of how he got run over by an airplane. Though not funny at the time, or during the long months of healing and therapy, the incident did become just another episode in what would one day be a major theme in Kiefer's life and career.

In May 1941, Dixie was sent off for duty on a most unusual ship: the USS *Wright* (AV-1). He was to be the ship's executive officer (XO), or second-in-command.

Named after aviation pioneer Orville Wright, Kiefer's new home was the navy's first and only "lighter-than-air aircraft tender." As it turned out, she had little to do with balloons or dirigibles but mostly served as a tender for seaplanes, as did her successors in the AV class. A tender is a vessel that services and supports other ships or, in *Wright*'s case, aircraft and aircraft carriers. When Dixie arrived aboard, the ship was already nearly twenty years old, having been commissioned in December 1921.

Kiefer was also swept up in a major strategic change of the time: President Roosevelt's decision to move Pacific Fleet Command from San Diego to Pearl Harbor, Hawaii. The transition was intended to be a signal

USS *Wright* (AV-1), a "lighter-than-air aircraft tender."

to the Japanese that the United States was serious about protecting her naval interests in the Pacific, and to try to discourage the nation from continuing her destructive advances throughout the region. Roosevelt preferred jawboning, influencing the Japanese diplomatically, since there was still a strong antiwar sentiment in America.

The eventual reaction by the Japanese was not what Roosevelt and the diplomatic community—or many in the military—had expected. The Empire would launch a surprise strike against the United States, not only in Hawaii at the new fleet headquarters location but also at other places where America had built up naval installations. They were convinced that such a preemptive attack would keep America from declaring war against Japan and, by treaty, Germany and Italy. And even if the United States did want to jump into the war after the strike, they would have few naval assets with which to attack an enemy as far away as the other side of the Pacific Ocean.

Dixie Kiefer and the *Wright* would play a major role in Roosevelt's deterrent buildup prior to the Pearl Harbor ambush. However, some of her crew might well have decided she was more a taxi or freighter than a warship as she crisscrossed the Pacific, transporting marines, construction workers, and aviation personnel. She also hauled cargo, including gasoline and other fuels, ammunition, and weapons, but mostly dull, boring construction materials. Typical destinations from Pearl Harbor included Wake Island, Johnston Island, Palmyra, and Midway.

It was late November 1941 when *Wright* left Pearl Harbor, bound first for Wake Island and then for the isolated Midway Atoll. As usual, they delivered gasoline—more than 63,000 gallons—to the base on Wake on November 28. They also carried construction workers and several high-ranking marine officers.

Among the passengers was one very important man—Captain Winfield Cunningham. He would be the officer in charge of all naval activities on Wake Island, his primary job being to complete the naval air station already under construction. However, Cunningham had clear orders not to spend a great deal of time and effort on air defenses. The Wake Island facility was meant to demonstrate to the Japanese that America was serious about protecting its Pacific interests. No one really thought the Empire would attack Wake—or any other outpost in the region, for that matter.

Next, Kiefer and the *Wright* headed for Midway. Because of that island's strategic position, many considered it one of the most important outposts in protecting American interests in the Pacific and on the West Coast of the United States. At Midway, Kiefer and his crew delivered mostly ammunition, along with putting ashore a large contingent of marines and several civilians. It was December 4 when the ship steamed away from the pier on Midway, ready for the 1,300-mile voyage back to Hawaii. It was a trip that would take more than three days and promised to be a boring crossing.

Little did they know.

At one point, the old seaplane-tender-turned-passenger-and-cargo-ship came unknowingly close to the Japanese striking force, on its way to launch the historic attack on Pearl Harbor. Though unaware at the time, *Wright* might have actually crossed the path of the Nippon fleet.

Of course, neither side knew about the existence of the other at the time. USS *Wright* would soon hear about what the Japanese had done, though. And once again, the news would alter the lives of hundreds of millions of people around the planet.

That certainly included Commander Dixie Kiefer. This close encounter east of Midway—halfway between Japan and the continental United States—was an insignificant precursor to a much more significant event, the first-ever sneak attack on America by a foreign power. The Sunday-morning bombing by the Japanese fleet would soon send Kiefer to another ship and then to the Coral Sea, the site of history's first naval battle in which neither fleet's vessels had ever laid eyes on the ships of the other.

The reason? The Battle of the Coral Sea would be conducted for the most part by Dixie Kiefer's cherished carrier-based airplanes. And Kiefer—as well as many of the pilots he had helped to train—would be a key player in the momentous clash.

Chapter Four

Coral Sea

It is now that we get to the main portion of our story, the events for which we have been laying the background so far, and for which Dixie Kiefer had been preparing himself during the previous busy and productive twenty-seven years of service in the US Navy.

By the time of the attack on Pearl Harbor, Dixie had fully developed his leadership style. We do not know all of his influences, but, as previously noted, he was blessed with persistence and self-motivation very similar to that of his grandfather Glade. He certainly had gotten plenty of on-the-job training in a variety of areas that would prove valuable, even including combat action at the tail end of World War I.

But there was another side of him that had to be a natural gift, and that was his friendly, easygoing demeanor, his ability to put himself on the level of the men he commanded and understand what they were experiencing. This was a trait that was not always appreciated by other military leaders.

Dixie did not seem to care. His men loved him. His immediate superiors saw and respected how he was able to get the most from a crew—not through rigid rules or tough supervision or arbitrary adherence to rules and protocol, but by inspiring his sailors and officers to do everything within their power to please him. They knew their commander was willing to jump in and do anything he required his men to do. Just as he had done when playing football as a young boy, and then again on the club team at the Naval Academy, he made sure they knew that they were all—from sailors to officers—players on the same team with the same objectives.

There were also early indications that Kiefer was not in step with how the military in general (and the navy in particular) treated minorities, especially African Americans. For the most part, they were used more as stevedores or lowly domestic help than trained fighting men. Blacks were more likely to be stewards, mess mates, and janitors than combat-ready sailors. But then, when a battle did occur, minorities in the navy were expected to man combat positions just like their shipmates, even though they had often received very little training.

As was the case with all branches of the armed forces, the navy was racially segregated—officially and practically—until President Truman ended the official part of that policy in 1948. Blacks lived, worked, and trained separately from their white counterparts until that year.

Early on, Kiefer made an effort to treat all of his men the same, to make certain black sailors were trained to fight just as their white counterparts were. His demeanor was the same toward all, regardless of their skin color. While the navy might have frowned on such behavior, and while this was a most unusual attitude for a naval officer of the time, Kiefer made it clear to all that he felt anyone in his squadron or aboard his ship was equal in all respects.

One sailor who served under Kiefer, Seaman 1st Class William Lent, later said, "Captain Kiefer was the most decent and compassionate man that ever lived. He treated everyone with dignity and equality."

Not many sailors would say that about an officer. Lent had several good reasons, though, including how his skipper would one day conduct himself in a particularly deadly situation. But he also had another anecdote that personified what kind of man Dixie Kiefer was.

One day aboard ship, Lent was standing in a long line waiting for chow. It was tropically hot, and the queue seemed endless. Then Lent realized the man who had walked up and was standing next to him was none other than his captain, Dixie Kiefer. The sailor, then just twenty-two years old, snapped to attention and saluted.

"At ease, sailor. Hotter than hell, ain't it, son?"

"Yes, sir."

"How long you been standing here?"

"Half an hour, I guess."

"What flavor ice cream you like?"

"Sir, chocolate . . ."

"Me, too. I'll be right back."

Kiefer double-timed to the head of the enlisted men's chow line, pulled rank to break in, got two chocolate ice-cream cones, and brought one of them back to Lent.

"Here you go, son. Keep up the good work."

Seaman William Lent, who is as of this writing still alive and in his mid-nineties, still remembers that incident. And he still tells anyone who will listen how much this simple gesture meant to him and all the men who witnessed it or heard about it. Many others would tell similar stories.

"General quarters! General quarters! All hands man battle stations! Man battle stations!"

For the first time, this particular crew of the USS *Wright* was called to take their positions for a potential real combat situation, not a drill. A simple return voyage back to Hawaii and a few days of liberty had just turned shockingly serious.

It was just after 0800 on the morning of December 7, 1941. Chaplains had been preparing for church services. Those who were off duty slept in, resting up for their arrival back at Pearl Harbor the next day at about dawn.

Then word came by radio that something unthinkable had happened. Was still happening. And not that far up ahead. This news sent everyone on the ship to their assigned battle stations.

The Japanese had sent waves of dive-bombers off carriers to the northwest and into the skies over the island of Oahu, viciously attacking airfields and other army and navy installations. They concentrated primarily on the battleships lined up along the piers at Ford Island, at Pearl Harbor. Details were still sketchy, but three facts soon became clear.

Two Japanese destroyers had also attacked the facilities at Midway that same day—shelling the place the *Wright* had just left, in addition to bombing the place toward which the ship now steamed.

Fellow navy personnel, fellow citizens, had died at both places.

The world was at war, and they were literally right in the middle of it.

The attack had caught the nation by surprise. The damage and loss of life was extensive. The very next day America would officially be at war with Japan as well as Germany and Italy. This was because of the Tripartite Pact between those three nations.

This was not merely a war. It was the Second World War.

Dixie Kiefer and the rest of the crew on the *Wright* did not have time to consider the ramifications of this shocking news. From what they could discern as they plowed on toward home port, they might well be seeing some of those Pearl Harbor attack aircraft returning to the ships from which they had taken off. Or the carriers that had delivered the deadly strike force might be sitting just over the horizon, waiting to retrieve their planes. The men on *Wright* had to be ready to launch an attack if they saw either—or defend against an assault should the Japanese spot them first.

As it turned out, they did not have to do either. They saw nothing.

It was a shocking vista for the crew when they steamed cautiously back into Pearl Harbor early on the morning of December 8. Fires still raged. Smoke billowed from Battleship Row. Rescue boats were still pulling survivors and bodies—mostly the latter—from the calm, oil-covered waters of the harbor. Nervous patrol boats and gun crews stood by while submarines patrolled just beyond the mouth of the harbor entrance, just in case there was another attack.

Thank goodness there had been no aircraft carriers at Pearl when the attack came. The US Navy only had three carriers in the Pacific at the time: the *Lexington*, the *Saratoga*, and the *Enterprise* (CV-6). *Lexington* and *Enterprise* had been conducting exercises near Wake Island. When news came of the attack, *Lexington* had launched search planes to try to find the Japanese attack fleet. They saw nothing. *Enterprise* had actually been scheduled to arrive back in Pearl on December 6, but bad weather had prevented her from being tied up at the pier there when the attack came. *Saratoga* had just left dry dock in Bremerton, Washington, where she had been for refitting. There were plans for her to stop in San Diego on her return trip to her home port. That is where she was, just entering the harbor at San Diego, when news came of the bombing.

When the Japanese attack force commanders learned that the carriers were at sea and not at Pearl Harbor, they almost made the decision to delay their long-planned assault until they could put the carriers out of service as well. However, they decided to go ahead with the attack as scheduled. After all, their primary targets were the battleships, and there they sat, lined up perfectly for a successful annihilation. The military leaders were convinced that destroying those warships would effectively end America's ability to threaten Japan's plans for empire building.

The choice not to delay the assault was one mistake that would soon come back to haunt the Japanese. So was their failure to bomb and put out of commission the base's repair and fuel storage facilities, as well as the submarines that were also right there for the taking. Japan's infatuation with battleships would cost them dearly over the next few years.

Meanwhile, everything had changed for the *Wright* and her crew, including her XO. However, nothing had changed when it came to the duties they were called upon to complete.

Everyone was now on a war footing. President Roosevelt had declared—and Congress had quickly backed him up—unlimited naval warfare. American warships were authorized to fire on any vessel flying the rising-sun Japanese flag. They were no longer required to follow previous "rules" of war at sea. A vessel did not have to be a warship to be considered a worthy target. American vessels were no longer obliged to approach a potential target, give fair notice that she was about to be attacked, and allow the vessel time to evacuate all its personnel. Now they could attack at will. Any aircraft spotted was a potential Japanese warplane. Only days after the attack, edgy antiaircraft gun crews had already taken down American planes by friendly fire.

However, the *Wright* was back to doing exactly what she had been doing before the planet tilted off its axis on December 7. Eleven days later, she was on her way again to Midway Atoll, carrying more than a hundred marines from the 4th Defense Battalion. There she was to take on board more than two hundred civilians, evacuating them back to

Hawaii. She safely made the round-trip and was back in Pearl Harbor the day after Christmas 1941.

USS *Wright* was due for repairs and remained in port until April. Then she was off to the South Seas and Australia, but without the man who had served as her XO for most of the past year.

When his ship arrived back in Pearl Harbor after the run to Midway, Dixie Kiefer received a dubious Christmas present. He was to report on February 11 aboard the relatively new aircraft carrier USS *Yorktown* (CV-5) as her new executive officer.

This ship was the first of the *Yorktown* class of flat tops and incorporated key changes learned from experiences with her predecessors, such as the *Lexington* and *Saratoga*. She had been laid down—the start of construction—in May 1934 in Newport News, Virginia; formally launched in April 1936 after being christened by her sponsor, First Lady Eleanor Roosevelt; and commissioned—placed into service—in September 1937.

USS *Yorktown* (CV-5) at anchor in Newport News, Virginia.

For the next four years, she and her sister carrier, the USS *Enterprise*, conducted exercises, duly impressing all involved with their performance. The first half of 1941 found her in the Atlantic. Though the United States was not involved with the war in Europe, *Yorktown* and other ships in the Atlantic Ocean maintained a war standing. Hitler had ordered his U-boats not to attack American warships, not wishing to draw America into the war just yet. But those US vessels were not aware of the decree. They had to be ready for anything.

On December 7, 1941, as Dixie Kiefer and the *Wright* were making their way back to Pearl Harbor from Midway, *Yorktown* was tied up in port at Norfolk, Virginia. As with so many other vessels, all plans for the flat top changed in a flash. Only nine days after Pearl and eight days after the declaration of war, the big carrier left her home port and headed for the Panama Canal, steamed on to San Diego, and quickly became part of Task Force 17 commanded by Admiral Frank Jack Fletcher. She soon saw her first action in the South Pacific, including extensive exploits in the successful raids—some of the very few events that could be considered a success so far in the war in the Pacific—on the Gilbert and Marshall Islands.

Dixie Kiefer joined *Yorktown* when she returned to Pearl Harbor in early February 1942. He reported to the ship's skipper, Captain Elliott Buckmaster. Dixie was pleased to learn that many of the pilots he had personally trained in Pensacola or directed at his various squadron command positions were among the fliers on his new ship. That included Joe Taylor, who was now not only a lieutenant commander but also in charge of the ship's Torpedo Squadron 3. Taylor and his team had already distinguished themselves in the assaults on the Gilbert Islands back in the first few days of February, the first real wounds inflicted against their foe.

Replenished and with her new XO, the carrier departed Hawaii on Valentine's Day, headed back to the war, bound for a body of water with the intriguing name of Coral Sea. There they were to meet up with Task Force 11, which had been built around one of Dixie's former billets, the USS *Lexington*.

Since before the United States had entered the war, the Japanese had continued a relentless move southward, capturing one island after another,

On the way to the war—and to pick up her new XO, Dixie Kiefer—*Yorktown* takes on a load of TBD-1 Devastator aircraft in San Diego.

seeking control of territory that could help with natural resources to fuel their expansion. After the December 7 attack, assuming the US Navy had little strike ability left with its battleships sunk or heavily damaged, they stepped up their land grab. They were clearly intent on eventually taking, or at least controlling, Australia along with the Philippine Islands, establishing an almost unbeatable regional empire.

As Kiefer and *Yorktown* headed southwest to assist in various operations, the Pacific Naval Command received strong intel that the Japanese were preparing to take Port Moresby, a key port on the southern coast of New Guinea. From there, the enemy would be much better able to control the seas—by air and by water—throughout the southern reaches of the South Pacific, including threatening Australia. This would be a crucial stop if the Allied forces could finally halt a strategic thrust southward by the Japanese.

Meanwhile, as the big flat top made her way southwestward, Dixie Kiefer was busy showing his new crew what kind of XO he intended to be. His first order was that nobody needed to wear any clothing any more formal than khaki shirts and pants. No neckties. It was just too damn hot where they were going.

Then, apparently with Captain Buckmaster's consent, Kiefer called a meeting of the officers and pointedly told them how he felt about things.

"I have become a commander in the Navy without so far making an asshole of myself. I'm convinced I can make admiral the same way. I sure intend to try." He looked around the room and saw mostly positive expressions on the officers' faces. "One more thing. It is my firm belief that an aircraft carrier should be operated for the benefit of and from the point of view of the air group. That's how I propose running things on *Yorktown*."

A few nights later, Kiefer himself got on the ship's bullhorn and asked all pilots to report to the wardroom (the officers' dining and recreation area).

Had their orders changed? What was going on?

When they stepped into the room, the first thing they saw was a big table completely covered with bottles of whiskey, procured from the medical officer's stores. There were also glasses with ice already in them. As he helped the stewards pour shots into glasses and hand them to the pilots, Dixie told them what this was all about.

"Boys, I know what it is like to fly around out there looking at nothing but haze and seawater. It can wear on a man's nerves." He held up a glass full of amber liquid and offered a toast: "Here's to the first meeting of the *Yorktown* Cocktail Club. We'll convene at least once a week. More often if it looks like our dispositions require it. Now, enjoy!"

Kiefer stuck to his word, too, with regular "meetings" for the pilots. He also made certain that the other crewmembers who flew aboard most of the planes on the carriers were not forgotten. The rear gunners were told that they had standing "prescriptions" at sick bay to get a shot of whiskey when they felt it necessary to calm their nerves.

After supporting several operations and being at sea for almost two months, *Yorktown* put into port on Tonga for upkeep and to take on stores. A crew of more than 2,200 men requires plenty of groceries. But when word came of the potential assault by the enemy on Port Moresby, the crew hastily completed their tasks and steamed away to rendezvous again with Task Force 11 and *Lexington* near the New Hebrides Islands (now Vanuatu).

They met up on the first day of May 1942.

Kiefer was about to become a major player in a truly historic battle, one that would leave military historians arguing over who actually won. A conflict in which the terms *tactical* and *strategic* would become operative. A clash that would absolutely establish that there had been a sea change in the nature of naval warfare.

It would also be a battle in which Dixie Kiefer would show the mettle of the man that he was, and why he was so loved and respected by his crew. That, and just how effective he was as a commander of men faced with brutal, bloody, fiery combat.

CHAPTER FIVE

Tactical and Strategic

FIRST, THOUGH, TWO MASSIVE OPPOSING FLEETS WOULD SPEND MOST OF a week darting about, futilely searching for each other in the confines of the Coral Sea.

Battles of this size and importance typically involve massive troop movements or intricate maneuvers by vessels in a fleet. This one was no exception. Because of the scale and the difficult-to-comprehend numbers involved, it is all too easy to overlook that it is individual human beings who enact such conflicts. Real individuals—sons, brothers, fathers, many of whom have never before faced such unimaginable stress, complicated situations, and sheer horror. It matters little whether the persons so caught up in the maelstrom have prepared for such an experience for decades or not at all. No one knows how he will do his job until called upon to perform under the most unimaginable conditions.

Some fail. Others do exactly what is expected of them. A few go above and beyond.

Dixie Kiefer would soon prove to be among the latter.

The lead-up to the Battle of the Coral Sea was mostly two great fleets frantically searching for the other in order to have the advantage of launching the initial strike. Both sides were reasonably sure the other was out there in the hazy mist and rumbling thunderstorms, but for three days neither could manage to locate the other.

Preparations began during the last days of April and the first of May 1942, when four different contingents of Japanese ships and troops got under way. The first was an invasion force, bound to capture Port

Moresby, New Guinea, the last bit of territory the Japanese Empire needed to control all of the big island.

The second enemy contingent was headed toward the small bit of land called Tulagi, in the Solomon Islands, to seize a good harbor, establish a seaplane base, and, from there, be able to support the New Guinea assault and future operations throughout the region, including hitting air bases in Australia. Only minimal resistance was expected from either of these targeted locations, Tulagi and Port Moresby.

The third group of ships, dubbed the "Covering Force," included the light aircraft carrier *Shoho*, six cruisers, a destroyer, and other support vessels. They were to take up a position between Tulagi and New Guinea to supply air cover, first for Tulagi, and then for the attack on Port Moresby.

Finally, the "Carrier Strike Force," which included the bigger Japanese flat tops *Zuikaku* and *Shokaku*, two heavy cruisers, and six destroyers. This impressive group of warships was to enter the Coral Sea south of Guadalcanal to support the invasion forces at both locations—but primarily Port Moresby—as well as to attack any Allied ships that might be foolish enough to rush to defend or attempt to recapture either outpost.

Meanwhile, Allied Task Forces 17 and 11, already in the Coral Sea, had come together as one unit after the meet-up on May 1 and were now collectively known as TF-17. Although intercepted coded messages further confirmed for HQ back in Pearl Harbor that the invasion plans were now in progress, neither they nor Admiral Fletcher were certain where the last and most dangerous force, the enemy's Carrier Strike Force, was, or when they might be swimming in the same pool with the Allied fleet. Nor did the Japanese know where the Allied carriers under Fletcher were. Both sides would eventually find out, almost simultaneously.

At any rate, by the first week of May 1942, the stage was set. The curtain went up when the Japanese, as expected, easily took Tulagi. Australians manning the garrison there evacuated ahead of the overwhelming invasion force. The Battle of the Coral Sea was officially under way—advantage: Japan.

On May 4, Fletcher hit the first lob over the net, ordering Buckmaster and Kiefer to take *Yorktown* and launch an assault on the invaders at Tulagi. They did just that, and it was a successful assault, abolishing a destroyer, two minesweepers, and several seaplanes. The young squadron leader Joe Taylor led his guys in with the first wave of attackers. But as impressive as the damage was, the Japanese still held the fine harbor after the shooting was over. They were launching seaplane missions from there just two days later.

Besides that, the attack had confirmed for the enemy that American carriers were now operating in the Coral Sea, and they had a good idea where one of them was. Search planes from the enemy Carrier Strike Force were sent to find *Yorktown*. However, the scouts guessed incorrectly where the big Allied carrier would be heading after the counterattack. They searched the wrong area and found nothing.

When Fletcher and his task force commanders received word that the Port Moresby invasion force had plans to launch the attack there on May 10, they wrapped up refueling—including topping off the tanks on *Yorktown* and her more than seven dozen aircraft—and prepared to intercept the Japanese light-carrier cover force several hundred miles to the northwest, well before the Japanese invasion force had reached their goal. The only oiler/tanker the Allied fleet had at its disposal at the time, the USS *Neosho* (AO-23), was sent—with a destroyer escort—a couple of hundred miles south, to avoid any danger of being damaged in the inevitable showdown. Fuel was crucial, not only to ships but also for the hundreds of aircraft that flew off the decks of the carriers. Fletcher obsessed about keeping his "floating gas station" out of harm's way.

Weather, more bad guesses, and blind luck kept each contingent of carriers from spotting the other. At one point, they were less than seventy nautical miles apart.

Meanwhile, even as they continued to look for Japan's two large carriers, Fletcher ordered the task force to steam northwest. He needed to be close enough to launch a major force off his own carriers' decks to throw a wrench into the Port Moresby invasion plans.

It was a nerve-wracking time for the men aboard *Yorktown* as well as *Lexington*. Planes flew off, conducted searches, and returned with little to report. After shooting real ammunition at Tulagi, there had been few other targets worthy of their attention. Just miles and miles of bumpy clouds, hail, rain, and fog, and the constant greenish-gray surface of the

Yorktown being refueled by the tanker USS *Neosho* (AO-23) in the Coral Sea, April 1942.

Coral Sea. That, and raw tension, which engulfed every man like the cloying tropical humidity.

One of *Yorktown*'s pilots, Lieutenant Commander Bill Burch, later said they had spent so much time patrolling the Coral Sea that they knew every flying fish by name. (Burch would receive two Navy Crosses for his action aboard *Yorktown*. He would also once again serve with Dixie Kiefer and experience with him a truly harrowing event, one for which he would once again be decorated for bravery by his country.)

Kiefer went out of his way to keep up the spirits of everyone he met. Many were shocked that their ship's second-in-command was most often down on the decks, moving around among them, talking, cheering them on, encouraging them to remain alert and ready. High-ranking officers typically remained on the bridge, speaking only to squadron leaders and other lower-rung commanders. Or spent off-duty time in the wardroom or their bunks. Commander Kiefer seemed to enjoy being with the sailors, the men who would do the bulk of the fighting when and if it ever came. He also drilled them incessantly, but in an encouraging way. He had them all convinced they could beat any son of a bitch if they worked hard and did what they had been trained to do.

Pilots and support crews alike on carriers for both sides in the potential showdown were poised and ready. So were their airplanes. They were prepared to begin dashing off flight decks the instant the carriers for the other side were spotted. There was an atmosphere of hair-trigger intensity so real it could be felt.

There was also a series of garbled messages; more wrong suppositions; plain old mistakes in latitude, longitude, and bearing; and still more frustrating errors that prolonged the agony and further heightened the intensity felt by every warrior on every vessel. But these men were humans. Well-trained humans, yes. But humans are not perfect.

Then, on May 7 at 0722, a Japanese scout plane reported back to his Carrier Strike Force that he had spotted one of the American carriers. There was no hesitation, no delay for a second scout's confirmation. The Japanese immediately launched all available aircraft and sent them in that direction. Finally!

Only when the first Zero fighter arrived did they realize the scout had actually mistaken the oiler *Neosho* and her escort for a flat top, more desired elements of the Allied task force. With almost eighty fighters and dive-bombers showing up, circling, the decision was made to go ahead and attack the only targets they had with half the planes they had dispatched. They sent the rest back to the carriers with their bombs, bullets, and torpedoes intact.

The escort destroyer, the USS *Sims* (DD-409), was brutally sunk in fifteen minutes. *Neosho* was seriously damaged, afire with thousands of gallons of fuel aboard, and the Japanese assumed she was done. The rest of the wave of fighters and dive-bombers hurried back to their respective carriers, just in case the big ships were already in the sights of the Allies. Just in case the oiler had been a deliberate decoy.

(The story of *Neosho* is one of the more inspiring, yet tragic, ones to come out of the Pacific War. Her crew managed to keep her afloat for more than four days, knowing she could explode or capsize at any moment, dumping them into shark-infested waters hundreds of miles from the nearest land. They were finally rescued. The ship was scuttled. Even so, more than one hundred men had abandoned the ship during the bombing and subsequent fires. Some died in the flaming oil, others drowned, and more were killed by sharks. Most ended up on life rafts and drifted away on the currents. Only four of them would be rescued nine days afterward, the rest succumbing to their wounds, exposure, or starvation.)

Now the Japanese Carrier Strike Force commander knew he had a problem. Another scout had located *Lexington* and *Yorktown* and their assorted support ships. They correctly surmised that the Allies were on their way to attack the Port Moresby Covering Force. But now the Japanese had no aircraft to go after them. They were all on their way back after rushing off in the opposite direction to attack *Neosho*. They would have to recover each of the planes that had been off on that wild goose chase—one at a time, of course—and then refuel every single one of them and re-arm half of them. However, it would be too late in the day by then to give chase. They would never catch the Allies in time to attack before nightfall. The best the Empire's navy had was toothless for the rest of the day. They would have to wait until the next morning to relocate the carriers and launch aircraft again.

Meanwhile, the American carriers had drawn within range and had located the Covering Force—now freed from protecting Tulagi—already in place to perform its second mission: shielding the assault on Port Moresby. As the Japanese had done when they believed they had finally spied an American carrier, the Allies ran off the decks of both flat tops every plane that would fly or had a pilot.

If there was any doubt about the importance of their objective, Admiral Frank Jack Fletcher settled it. As his pilots and gunners ran to their aircraft, he got on the speakers to implore them to "get that goddamned carrier!"

The *Lexington*'s aircraft were, by design, in the air first, followed closely by those from *Yorktown*. Lieutenant Commander Joe Taylor had settled in and was buckling up to lead the *Yorktown* force away and do his admiral's bidding. Then, seconds before they were to taxi over and zoom off the deck, Taylor noticed that someone had climbed up onto the wing of his plane and was leaning into his cockpit.

It was Dixie Kiefer.

"Joe, if this doesn't keep you safe and bring you back, nothing will," Dixie told him, as he stuck something to the plane's instrument panel with a piece of cellophane tape. It was a four-leaf clover with a few strands of red hair wrapped around it.

"The hair belongs to a mysterious redhead. And it only increases the charm's lucky powers." Kiefer grinned and slapped Taylor on the shoulder before he jumped down from the wing.

On the way back to the bridge, Dixie paused and spoke to one of the flight officers.

"If that kid doesn't make it back, it'll destroy my faith in humanity."

Joe Taylor and William Burch aboard *Yorktown* while in the Coral Sea.

Just after 1000 that morning, even as the Japanese carrier-based planes were sinking the *Sims* and pummeling *Neosho*—the ill-fated oiler and escort—Taylor's planes and the rest of the Allied force launched a fierce attack of their own on the Japanese light carrier *Shoho*. The enemy flat top still had most of her aircraft below the flight deck, preparing to cover the invasion or to attack Task Force 17 should the Allies be located.

Planes off *Lexington* struck first and struck hard, disabling the carrier and leaving her powerless. *Yorktown*'s pilots finished her off. Once the Japanese received word of the loss of *Shoho* and were aware that they had no air cover, the enemy invasion force made a broad U-turn and raced back to the north, delaying—and ultimately ending—the plans to take Port Moresby.

Only two planes from *Lexington* and one from *Yorktown* were lost. One of the pilots, *Lexington* dive-bomber squadron commander Robert E. Dixon, broke radio silence only long enough to famously send a terse, predetermined coded message back to the fleet: "Scratch one flat top! Signed, Bob."

The Allies—elements from Australia and other friendly nations were a part of the task force by then—were elated. They had struck a first major blow! True, the Allies had lost a tanker and a destroyer. However, for the first time in the war, six months in, the Allies had halted Japan's seemingly unstoppable drive southward. And an enemy aircraft carrier with its entire complement of planes—even if it was only a light carrier and a total of eighteen aircraft—was now at the bottom of the Coral Sea.

Advantage: United States and her partners.

Dixie Kiefer was waiting on the flight deck as each returning plane landed. He personally greeted as many of the crewmembers as he could with a grin and a slap on the back. Then, when Joe Taylor pounced down and stopped, Kiefer ran over to where he was climbing down onto the wing. He grabbed Taylor and locked him in a bear hug.

Everyone was more than aware, though, that there were other, far more lethal enemy ships out there somewhere. Fletcher and the commanders knew by then that their oiler had been attacked by a significant number of planes, almost certainly off carriers. They had no idea whether *Neosho* remained afloat and if she would be available to

USS *Yorktown* flight deck at sunrise in the Coral Sea, May 1942.

keep their fuel tanks topped off. A destroyer was already on the way to find her—or her oil slick. Scout planes off both Allied carriers were now back in the air, searching desperately, knowing that the Japanese, because of the *Shoho* attack, could draw a bead on where in the Coral Sea those attackers likely took off.

As he wandered over the ship, checking readiness and encouraging his boys, Dixie Kiefer knew the next day would probably—and finally— bring them into contact with the enemy's two big carriers. And, of course, the deadly birds that nested the night on their decks. If, during his mean- derings, he wandered into the ready room for Torpedo Squadron Five, he might have heard his protégé, Joe Taylor, talking to his pilots.

"*Lexington* led the way today, boys, and we finished her off. Tomor- row it'll be us," Taylor told them. "Fact is, we will have one hell of a job on our hands. And there's a damned good chance only a few of us will be coming home. But let's pack 'em in the way we did today."

Had he heard Taylor's speech, Kiefer would surely have been proud. No one knew better than he that the next day would be a crucial one in the fight to blunt Japan's war effort. But he would have been realistic enough, just as his student was, to know it would be a monstrous challenge.

The next morning, it was another pilot (one whose radio malfunctioned during his report) and then Bob Dixon—he of the terse good news about *Shoho*—the commander of *Lexington*'s Scouting Squadron 2, who finally spotted what they all had been looking for.

"Report two carriers, two battleships, four heavy cruisers, several destroyers. One hundred seventy miles north but heading southwest at top speed toward the fleet," he quickly radioed.

"Pilots, man your planes! Pilots, man your planes!"

The call on the ship's loudspeakers sent everyone scurrying. They had found their objective. Now they needed to be in the air and on the way. If they had found the Japanese, and if they were coming fast, the Japanese had likely found the Allies. Any plane not in the air could be much more easily destroyed should the enemy already be launching their own aircraft.

Their supposition was correct. It is one of the interesting aspects of this battle that both sides, after floundering around for days in the hot, humid Coral Sea, spotted each other at almost the same instant.

Joe Taylor was one of those pilots hustling to his Douglas TBD Devastator torpedo bomber. He knew the others in his squadron, as well as his rear gunner/radioman, were right behind him, just as anxious as he was to get their plane's wings unfolded, move out on the flight deck, and get airborne.

Then, once in the sky, all the aircraft were meeting up in predetermined formation before heading off through fog and thunderheads toward their targets. To a man, they were motivated in part by revenge. The two aircraft carriers they were so determined to sink this tropical morning had been a part of the Pearl Harbor attack force five months earlier. Many of the pilots and planes they would inevitably encounter that day had dropped bombs and torpedoes at that peaceful place on an otherwise quiet Sunday morning.

Those men would exact no small amount of retribution over the next few hours. But there would be losses, too. And the enemy planes and their skilled and religiously determined pilots would do plenty of damage as well.

In the end, it would be up to military tacticians and historians to determine who won and who lost this match.

The consensus? It was a tactical win for the Japanese. They would sink one of the carriers in the Allied task force and seriously impair the other, while the Allies would only manage to do damage to (but not sink) one of the Empire's flat tops, the *Shokaku*. There was no damage done to their other carrier.

However, the Japanese would lose significant numbers of pilots and gunners as well as the planes they flew off their carriers' decks. In addition, the *Shokaku* was damaged badly enough and the *Zuikaku* had lost so many planes and required such heavy-duty replenishment that both were forced out of service for the next several months. That meant neither was available for another crucial showdown that was coming up only about a month after the action in the Coral Sea.

That, plus the fact that a light carrier belonging to the Japanese had been sunk and the land grab by the emperor's troops had been stopped cold, gave the Allies a strategic win.

Regardless, on the morning of May 8, 1942, Commander Dixie Kiefer, the XO of the USS *Yorktown*, was not interested in tactical-versus-strategic calculations. He had just sent off from his ship over a hundred young men, many of whom were like sons to a man who had never had children. They were off to a brutal showdown in the middle of a stormy sea. He also knew that at that very moment there were likely a hundred or more Japanese pilots and gunners headed his way with the intent of sending *Yorktown* and *Lexington* to the bottom.

After watching the last Devastators and Dauntlesses disappear into the gathering rain squalls, he turned and headed up to the bridge to do what he could to ensure the best possible outcome from whatever the hell was about to happen.

Chapter Six

"I'll Show You How to Handle This Ship!"

THE UNUSUAL OCCURRENCES OF THE BATTLE OF THE CORAL SEA continued throughout its most intense days—May 7 and 8—as *Yorktown*, Dixie Kiefer, the ship's crew, and its flying squadrons watched and fought, fired and dodged bombs and bullets and torpedoes, ate, slept, treated wounded, and made hundreds of life-and-death decisions. Many years later, an admiral who had studied the various actions of the day declared, "Without a doubt, May 7, 1942, vicinity of Coral Sea, was the most confused battle area in world history." The commander of the Japanese carrier fleet later told his superiors that what he experienced during those two days caused him to vow to quit the navy if he survived the inevitable showdown.

Half a day before the fleets had found each other, planes from *Yorktown* and *Lexington* met and surprised some of their Japanese counterparts in the skies between the two fleets. They promptly had themselves a spirited dogfight. Nine enemy planes splashed. The Allies lost three.

In the late afternoon of May 7, at least six different Japanese aircraft on the way back from trying to find the American carriers became disoriented. They apparently mistook *Yorktown*'s decks for their own mother ship and tried to land. Two of them were shot down, and the CV-5's gun crews chased away the others.

The really serious business would start the next morning after each group spotted the other and launched attacks. *Yorktown*'s planes, led by Taylor and Burch, among others, quickly located and put two bomb holes in the flight and hangar decks of *Shokaku*. The blasts reached a

Dauntless SBD-5 scout bombers prepare to roll off the deck of USS *Yorktown*.

gasoline storage tank, starting a big fire, and put an engine service shop out of business. Though not in danger of sinking, this damage ensured the enemy carrier would not be able to launch any more aircraft. It also meant they would not be able to recover those that came back from their own attacks on the Allied flat tops. They would have to find land bases at which to put down or, if they could not make it there, ditch their planes in the sea. Meanwhile, the *Zuikaku* ran off and hid in a raging thunderstorm. It was a shrewd move, as she escaped damage.

Back at Task Force 17, the Japanese had shown up at about 1100 hours and immediately put to use their pent-up frustration, launching wave after wave of determined, high-speed attacks.

However, the Allied carriers' gun crews, those on the escorts, and the cover patrol aircraft were much better equipped than their predecessors had been. And they were just as thrilled to finally be able to strike a blow.

Over the next hour, they successfully deflected most of their attackers and put many of the "Kates" and "Vals"—nicknames for the Japanese torpedo bombers and dive-bombers—into the drink.

Inevitably, some enemy aircraft did manage to get through *Lexington*'s near-continuous hail of gunfire. Three bombs and two torpedoes found a home. The damage was heavy, but her crew found a way to keep her under power. They were even able to continue to land and take off aircraft throughout most of the assault. Unfortunately, they were unaware that a gas tank belowdecks was leaking fumes. Later, just when the *Lexington*'s crew thought they had saved their ship, a spark set off a major fire and gas explosion. The big ship had to be abandoned. Once all survivors were off and safe, her demise was hastened by shells from an accompanying Allied destroyer.

Yorktown, with Buckmaster and Kiefer on the bridge, fared a bit better.

At least eight torpedoes were seen heading her way during the height of the enemy battering. Each time, the big ship managed to make surprisingly agile course corrections and dodge them. At one point, the helmsman was a tad slow to make an ordered hard turn. Captain Buckmaster suddenly pushed him out of the way and grabbed the wheel from him.

"Give me that wheel! I'll show you how to handle this ship!"

Sure enough, with a mighty effort, the skipper sent the carrier into a remarkably sharp zig. The torpedo was observed as it just missed its massive but elusive target and zoomed on past. The weapon would eventually sink harmlessly to the bottom of the sea.

Dixie Kiefer turned and winked at the others whose general quarters assignments had them on the ship's bridge. Such a display of bravado was decidedly uncharacteristic of Buckmaster, an old-line skipper. Close call or not, Kiefer and some of the others found some humor in their captain's impulsive break in the usual chain of command.

The CV-5 did not get through the attack unscathed. One bomb did find *Yorktown*'s flight deck, exploding in the infrastructure below. Sixty-six men were either seriously wounded or killed. Two other bombs did damage as well.

It would be months before the paperwork caught up, but Dixie Kiefer would be awarded the first of several medals for his leadership

Crewmen assess damage to *Yorktown*'s third and fourth decks after hits taken at the Battle of the Coral Sea.

and valor. He would receive in October 1942 the Distinguished Service Medal for the way he prepared his crew to fight in the Battle of the Coral Sea. The text of the citation reads:

> *The President of the United States of America takes pleasure in presenting the Navy Distinguished Service Medal to Commander Dixie Kiefer (NSN: 0-34685), United States Navy, for exceptionally meritorious and distinguished service in a position of great responsibility to the Government of the United States as Executive Officer of the U.S.S. YORKTOWN (CV-5) in preparation for, during, and after battle. By his sound judgment, thorough planning and indefatigable zeal, unbounded enthusiasm and courageous example, he contributed greatly toward bringing his ship and her Air Group to the high state of desire to engage the enemy and her readiness for battle which enabled the Air Group to make three successive attacks on the enemy at Tulagi on 4 May 1942, to attack and sink an enemy carrier on 7 May 1942, and to attack and seriously*

damage an enemy carrier and to engage and destroy many enemy aircraft on 8 May 1942, and to hold to a minimum the damage received from an aerial bomb and many near misses, and finally, which enabled the ship and Air Group to come through these actions with aggressive fighting spirit undiminished.

The citation was signed, "For the President, James Forrestal, Acting Secretary of the Navy." It would not be the last such honor that Forrestal, the native of Beacon, New York, would bestow on Dixie Kiefer.

Also, in the aftermath of battle, there was about to be yet another example of how Kiefer seemed to intuitively know how to get his men through one traumatic event and prepare for another.

Throughout the afternoon of May 8, the crew assisted the wounded even as they fought to control fires and fix what damage they could. They also worked to get returning planes back onto the flat top and safely to the hangar deck, sending others off to patrol, preparing all of them to go right back out if ordered to do so. In addition, they had landed as many of the planes off *Lexington* as they could manage once the decision was made to abandon and sink her. The flying crews were dog-tired from their two days of attacks on the enemy and skirmishes with Japanese aircraft, but they grabbed coffee, took catnaps, and were ready for the call, should it come. All this was done knowing at any time there could be another attack roaring down at them from the sky or sneaking up on them from below.

Then word came that both Japanese carriers appeared to have turned and were heading north, away from the Allies. Admiral Fletcher, TF-17 commander, still was not certain the battle was over. He was well aware, however, that he had one carrier heavily damaged—he did not yet know it would get worse for *Lexington* very soon—and, as usual, he was worried about fuel problems since his precious tanker was missing and feared sunk. He decided to withdraw to the south and west and eventually, when approved, to possibly make for Pearl Harbor and its repair facilities. Fletcher suspected there would be upcoming action that would require as many aircraft carriers as they could get in the water. He had no idea it would be so soon, and so crucial.

Indeed, the Japanese Carrier Strike Force had decided to retreat. Their damaged flat top was on its way out of the Coral Sea as soon as the Allied attack subsided, and the other was now out from beneath the thunderstorm and following close behind. They were under the impression that both American aircraft carriers as well as a tanker and destroyer had been sunk. Part of that withdrawal decision was fuel-related as well. But the Carrier Strike Force commander was most concerned because he had lost between 30 and 40 percent of his airplanes and their very experienced crews. Not only did he doubt he could launch an adequate defense cover force, but he also knew he did not have enough birds in the coop to carry out any worthwhile offense.

Late that afternoon, with the sun dipping low in a bright-red sky back toward Australia and the Great Barrier Reef, with *Lexington* afire and sending up billows of black smoke in the distance, Dixie Kiefer called a meeting of the *Yorktown* Cocktail Club. All the surviving aircraft crewmembers and as many of the ship's officers as could attend—those who were not on duty—found the wardroom especially well stocked with "medicinal" alcoholic beverages.

It was a somber gathering. For his part, Kiefer could see his former ship in trouble on the horizon, the vessel on which he began duty the ominous week of the 1929 stock market crash. More than two hundred men had died in the attack on the *Lexington* and would soon go down with her when she was scuttled, buried at sea along with their ship. Dixie also knew by name many of the dead and injured from *Yorktown*'s crew—from which small city they hailed, what they planned to do when this damn war was over. He had personally joked with and slapped the backs of each and every one of the pilots and rear-seat guys who had not come back that day. He even knew many of the flight crew members over on *Lexington* and had to be wondering who had survived the day and who had not.

Even so, Dixie Kiefer was a shrewd enough observer of human emotion that he knew this club meeting was a necessity. There could be more action at any moment. Men still manned guns on his ship's deck. There would definitely be more hostilities in the coming weeks. They might eventually have to fight their way all the way back to Hawaii if they received orders to get their ship fixed there. Kiefer somehow knew these brave boys needed a pick-me-up, a break, a cathartic get-together to decompress from the tension of the past few days. The men who shared whiskeys and honest talk that afternoon in *Yorktown*'s wardroom would never forget it. For the rest of their days, they would tell others about Kiefer's cocktail party and what it meant to them.

At the end of the "meeting," when they broke up and went back to their cots or returned to duty, they had decided to a man that even though they and their ship might have taken a punch to the jaw, they were not down for the count.

They and their ship had survived to fight another day.

CHAPTER SEVEN

Turnaround

THE BLIND-SIDE BOMBING OF PEARL HARBOR HAD NOT HAD THE result the Japanese expected. Instead of keeping the United States out of the war and crippling any potential naval effort in the Pacific, the attack did just the opposite. Even though the battleships had been damaged or sunk as intended, the Americans found they could fight just fine, thank you, with carriers, airplanes, destroyers, cruisers, and submarines. They proved it in the Coral Sea and were proving it every day with submarines, despite the Silent Service's problems with their torpedoes malfunctioning. The Allies had even bombed the Home Islands—the Doolittle Raid—in April 1942, using big bombers off the deck of the USS *Hornet* (CV-8). The physical damage of that raid was minimal, but the psychological effect—if the Allies could bomb Tokyo, they could kill the sacred leader of the country, Emperor Hirohito—was earth-shaking.

By the spring of 1942, the Japanese controlled much of the South Pacific, including the Philippines, Singapore, and Malaysia. The master plan—to own the Indian Ocean and meet up in the Suez with Field Marshal Erwin Rommel and the Germans along with the Italians—was successfully under way. But despite the blow struck at Pearl Harbor, the United States was now threatening Japan from the east.

The answer, the Empire felt (though not unanimously), was to strike back by first taking the strategically placed outpost of Midway Atoll, a key Allied base and landing/refueling spot literally halfway between the US mainland and the Japanese Home Islands. Construction was already in progress to make it a vital submarine base, too, extending the range of those boats tremendously.

From there, the Imperial Japanese Navy (IJN) could potentially move on to more attacks on Hawaii, in the Aleutians, and even against the North American west coast, ideally demoralizing the reluctant Americans and chasing them out of the war. Taking Midway would be a major step in their strategy, and, indeed, such an attack was already in the planning stages as early as December 1941. Briefings had even been conducted already on bombing runs against aircraft factories in Los Angeles.

Unbeknownst to the IJN, the Americans had been reading their mail. In May 1942, the Allies were reasonably aware from intercepted and translated code transmissions that Midway was to be the target of a major assault, one that would include as many as four Japanese aircraft carriers and a huge invasion fleet for which they would provide air cover. Then ground forces would go ashore and take what would be left of the tiny islands that made up Midway. In addition to planned dates and times, the Allies knew the Japanese had included in the operation intricate plans to lure more American carriers into a trap and put them out of business, just as they still believed they had done with two flat tops in the Coral Sea a month before. This was a major goal of IJN commander Isoroku Yamamoto. He was convinced the US carriers were the greatest threat to his own navy and could be virtually eliminated as part of the Midway operation.

Instead, with advance knowledge, the Allies had the opportunity to prepare their own snare. Even so, everyone was aware that this forewarning only offered limited advantage. They still had little time and precious few assets to prepare for the face-off against far superior forces.

Admiral Chester Nimitz—who, like Dixie Kiefer, was of German descent and from the middle of the continent, a Texas native—was the commander of what the United States had by then named the "Pacific Ocean Areas." He knew Midway falling into enemy hands would be a potential mortal blow to the US war effort. Losing was not an option.

Despite considerable doubt from his own commanders, who did not believe Japan would take the risk and commit the resources to take an isolated garrison like Midway, Nimitz decided to trust what his intelligence people were telling him. He set about preparing for an all-out enemy assault on the atoll. He promptly recalled USS *Enterprise* and USS *Hornet* back to Pearl Harbor for replenishment, along with any necessary repairs, and to pick up a full complement of aircraft, ready to defend Midway. And he told the survivor of Coral Sea, the *Yorktown*, to hurry on back. Those three ships were all he had in the way of aircraft carriers. Navy intelligence was certain the Japanese had four carriers on the way toward Midway.

And, by the way, *Yorktown* presented a bit of a problem. She arrived at Pearl on May 27 and went directly to the repair facility dry dock. Original estimates done while she was en route were that it would take three months to get her bomb damage repaired and have her ready to fight again. Plus, they would need to somehow replace aircraft and crews lost in the battle.

A damaged *Yorktown* in dry dock at Pearl Harbor after the Battle of the Coral Sea.

Crewmembers had conflicting emotions. They were still anxious to go out and help beat Japan, to avenge the loss of their shipmates. But three months' downtime likely meant stateside leave. They, of course, had no idea of the reasons for a quicker turnaround. They just knew they were well overdue for some rest.

Admiral Nimitz, along with the leadership aboard the carrier, balked at the body-shop estimate. Nimitz even put on wading boots and sloshed around in the water not yet completely drained from the dry dock, inspecting the damage for himself. The admiral and his fellow officers demanded a better result from all to get the carrier back into the war.

Okay, they said, three weeks—but that would be pushing it.

"You will have her ready to sail in one week, alongside *Hornet* and *Enterprise*," the admiral declared.

Fortunately, damage to the elevators—the massive lifts that carried planes from the hangar deck on the ship's second level up and down from the flight deck above—was not as bad as first thought. The big hole the bomb had punched in the flight deck turned out to be a relatively minor patch if they ignored noncritical damage below.

Toiling around the clock, yard workers finished the repairs well ahead of even the seemingly impossible Nimitz pronouncement. Special arrangements were made with the Hawaiian Electric Company to conduct rolling power blackouts in order to supply the unprecedented amount of electricity required for the repair effort. Shortcuts were made. For example, ruptured seams in the hull were not re-welded, as would normally be the process. Instead, huge metal plates were used to cover the breaks, and those were welded into place.

This rapid turnaround would confuse the Japanese. They were still under the impression that *Yorktown* had been sunk in the Coral Sea, just as her sister carrier had been. In the upcoming battle, they continuously called her by the wrong name, assuming it was some other ship.

We have no record of what Dixie Kiefer did during this time and whether he got to see his mother or sister. It is unlikely, since he would more likely have remained with the ship, helping to oversee the work. He also had to supervise the arrival of a bunch of new aircraft and crewmembers who were sent over from another carrier they were expecting to arrive, one that had been in refit on the mainland and was just then heading back toward Pearl Harbor. She would not be able to get to Pearl, get ready, and make it to Midway in time for the upcoming party, but her planes certainly could. Some of *Lexington*'s flight crews shipped over as well. It was a duke's mixture of men from an array of previous duty, which would quickly become problematic.

Unbelievably, *Yorktown* was back out of the gate at Pearl Harbor on the morning of May 30, 1942, as part of TF-17. That was only three days after showing up at the dry dock—a wonderful example of how quickly the unsung heroes in the repair facilities could get things done. This was seemingly an impossible turnaround, even if the ship had only taken on food and supplies and new aircraft, not to mention having to undergo repairs from an enemy bomb attack.

(The story of the raising and salvage efforts for the damaged and sunken battleships hit on December 7 is another inspiring story. Men—and women—who never fired a shot in battle contributed mightily to the eventual victory, but with hammers, saws, and welding torches instead of bullets.)

Yorktown did still have work crews aboard, finishing up repairs as the big carrier put Pearl Harbor behind her and started the 2,100-mile trip to a location in the Pacific Ocean north of Midway Atoll. The assigned position for the carriers to rendezvous had been designated "Point Luck." And they would certainly need some. The damaged carrier was only able to run at reduced speed and could really do little more than launch and recover aircraft. Still, that would have to be enough.

There were morale issues, too. This was normal, considering the tension and stress of the past six months. That, and the realization that the crew was once again going into combat with no leave time contributed to the problem. Also, because of the mixed-up assortment of patched-together flight squadrons, several units renamed and renumbered after being pulled together from other ships, and their crews being required to perform unfamiliar duty—dive-bombers were now scouts, torpedo bombers were made dive-bombers, all according to need—there were inevitably some raw feelings.

It got even worse when many of the *Yorktown*'s disparate flight crews descended on the Ford Island Officers' Club for a party before shipping out. The management called the Shore Patrol when the group became rowdy, and they were threatened with brig time and courts-martial because they were not wearing the required neckties, as per Dixie Kiefer's relaxed rules.

Kiefer found his morale-building talents sorely challenged, but he did his best. When he was not supervising repairs, he was doing all he could to build a team on *Yorktown*. The men got away from the officers' club debacle with no formal charges, and, in retrospect, the incident might actually have helped pull them closer together. The fliers were soon getting along better, aware they would all be on the same side against whatever force they were about to face.

Meanwhile, on Midway, the navy, the army air force, and the marines had assembled more than 115 aircraft, ready to go. To the west, the Japanese forces were steaming rapidly toward the atoll at the same time. As it turned out, they were moving too fast. Trying to once again take advantage of the element of surprise—unaware that the Allies knew all along that they were coming—the primary members of the enemy fleet left behind some important elements in their haste. For example, they did not allow time for picket submarines to get in place. This oversight meant that the three US carriers were able to move into position at Point Luck without being spotted and reported. That would prove to be a major factor in the eventual outcome of the battle.

On June 3, based on a report that the main Japanese force had been spotted exactly where and when navy intelligence had predicted, nine B-17 bombers flew off Midway's airstrip to try to dissuade them from coming any closer. Though the planes dropped every bomb they carried, they hit nothing.

That night, just after midnight, a PBY seaplane from Midway spotted a Japanese oiler and launched a torpedo in its direction. It struck and did damage. No one knew at the time, but this would be the only successful airplane-launched torpedo strike in the Battle of Midway. If they had known this fact, anyone knowledgeable about air tactics would have declared that there was no way the Allies could hope to win this battle with such a stunning lack of success.

At 0430 on the morning of June 4, the Japanese launched a full-scale and fierce attack on the tiny atoll. There were heavy losses on both sides, but when the smoke cleared, Midway was still there, still capable of fighting back. The runway was clear and usable. Planes could still refuel. Air defense weapons were, for the most part, still in service, and deadly. The last Japanese pilots to vacate the area reported that there would have to be another air assault before their marines could ultimately go ashore and claim the two main (but tiny) islands.

Meanwhile, another flock of torpedo bombers off Midway had launched an attack on elements of the Japanese contingent—again, with little damage done.

The Japanese task force commander now had a quandary. He knew the American aircraft carriers should be arriving on the scene at any moment, but so far, they had inexplicably not launched an attack. He also knew the Midway land-based aircraft could continue to refuel, reacquire bombs and torpedoes, and come after his fleet before he could pound them again. They might be more successful the next time around in hitting his ships—especially his vital carriers.

Should he arm his planes for an attack on the so-far-invisible American aircraft carriers, assuming they could be located? Or should he follow his air squadron commanders' recommendation that he once again attack the atoll and then send marines ashore to secure it? And worry about the American carriers and their aircraft later, assuming another land assault would lure them into the fray?

All this while, Dixie Kiefer and the three US ships waited, though not very patiently. Waited for the Japanese to show their hand. For them to either come after their ships or try to invade Midway. Or both.

The longer they waited, and the more they heard about how ineffective the Midway-based bombers had been so far, the more Kiefer and his crew wanted to fly down there and do some damage.

Their chance would come sooner rather than later.

Chapter Eight

Dixie's Gallant Swim

If either side in the Battle of Midway had known for certain what their opponent had, neither would have considered it a fair fight. The Japanese forces included eighty-six warships to the Americans' twenty-seven. The Imperial Japanese Navy contingent had eleven battle-ships, including the massive *Yamato*. The United States had none. Zero. There were fifty-three destroyers heading eastward from Japan. The force assembled by the Allies had only seventeen.

Only in aircraft carriers were the forces close to equal. The Japanese brought only four, though plans were originally to have at least three more. The light carrier *Shoho* had been sunk in the Coral Sea. The big carrier *Shokaku* had been damaged by fliers off *Lexington* and *Yorktown*—though no worse than *Yorktown* had been—but she was still in dry dock under-going repairs. *Zuikaku* did not receive a scratch in the Coral Sea, but she had lost many planes and their flight crewmembers. Getting replacements for both proved to be a slow process, so she, too, was unavailable for what the Japanese were calling Operation MI—the taking of Midway Atoll.

The Americans would counter with three flat tops. Since this show-down would ultimately be conducted mostly in the air, this equality in carriers would play a major role in the outcome of the Battle of Midway.

All available Japanese aircraft were, of course, based on the four flat tops, *Kaga*, *Akagi*, *Hiryu*, and *Soryu*, each of which had taken part in the attack on Pearl Harbor. The count was 325 planes. The United States had brought along 233 carrier-based airplanes. But with an additional 115 aircraft in place on Midway, the total for the Americans was 348, an advantage of two dozen planes. In a close battle, that might be enough to make a difference.

Even so, the element of surprise would soon play an even bigger role. Admiral Raymond Spruance, the commander of Task Force 16—which included the carriers *Enterprise* and *Hornet*—had sent a short communiqué to headquarters, saying, "If the presence of [the carriers] remains unknown to enemy we should be able to make surprise flank attack on enemy carriers from position northeast of Midway. Further operations will be based on result of these attacks, damage imposed by Midway forces, and information of enemy movements."

Dixie Kiefer and his *Yorktown* flight crews clearly had a major role in this particular drama. So far, though, the only planes off her decks were scouts, trying to find the enemy carriers. As was his nature, Kiefer made his rounds, encouraging the young fliers, but also cheering on the hangar and flight-deck sailors. Their jobs would be crucial, getting as many airplanes in the air as quickly as possible once word came. Recovering those who managed to come back. And being ready to aim and shoot the ship's protective guns, too, when the Japanese inevitably launched a counterattack.

Maybe doing all three chores at once.

The stocky Kiefer was in constant motion, up and down the decks, on the bridge, in the ready rooms. His grin and upbeat nature were contagious, just as they had been in the Coral Sea confrontation. His job got a little more difficult when word came that the first waves of attackers would start rolling off *Hornet* and *Enterprise* at 0750 on the morning of June 4. More planes were simultaneously launched from Midway, too. *Yorktown*'s crews were to be held in reserve, in case there were other carriers or targets.

"You'll get your chance! Be ready!" Kiefer repeated to every man he saw, keeping them alert and ready despite their disappointment.

Sure enough, they got their call at just after 0900, about an hour later. Twelve torpedo bombers, seventeen dive-bombers, and six Wildcats were quickly airborne and forming up to go after the enemy carriers.

Airplanes from all three US carriers at first had difficulty finding the enemy ships. The Pacific is a big ocean. Then, when the enemy vessels were finally located, the Americans launched a deliberately uncoordinated attack, sacrificing orderliness for quickness and surprise. Fuel quickly became an issue since the IJN forces were so far from Point Luck. Most US fighters had to retreat when they ran low on gas, leaving attackers without cover. Many of the torpedo bombers had to ditch when they ran out of fuel. Ten of *Yorktown's* one dozen relatively slow, unarmored, and unescorted Devastator torpedo bombers were shot down, both by Japanese Zero fighter aircraft and by guns on the carriers and other vessels. The few torpedo planes that did get through the barrage missed, or else their fish failed to explode, an issue the torpedo bombers shared with submarines.

Back at the *Yorktown*, Captain Buckmaster and his XO were only able to get spotty reports of what was happening. They did not sound good.

Though doing little to damage the enemy carriers, those initial torpedo attacks did cause the Japanese to spend their time and efforts avoiding them and using a great deal of their fuel and ammunition to repel the TBDs. The IJN carriers and their escort ships were so occupied with the torpedo bombers—including a squadron from *Yorktown*—that they did not see an attack force of dive-bombers from *Enterprise* and *Yorktown* zooming in from behind them.

The attack came at a most inopportune time for the Japanese carriers. Preparing to launch their own planes, already heavily armed, to go after the American flat tops, the hangar deck was covered with tight lines of aircraft, in-use fuel hoses, and bombs and other ammunition, all out in the open, being loaded onto airplanes. The ships were at their most vulnerable.

Akagi took only one direct hit, but the bomb settled into the hangar deck, igniting gasoline and setting off bombs stacked and ready to attach to aircraft. The big ship was ablaze from bow to stern within minutes. The *Yorktown* dive-bomber squadron went after *Soryu*, hitting with at least three 500-pound bombs and inflicting major carnage. After dropping their bombs, some of the planes in the squadron circled back and flew cover for the others, using their guns to strafe the decks, causing even more fires and killing enemy sailors. *Kaga*, too, was struck multiple times and was quickly ablaze. Only *Hiryu* survived with no damage the sudden onslaught of American dive-bombers. The other three Japanese carriers would ultimately be abandoned and scuttled, sunk, out of the war.

The first US carrier–based bomber attack came at 0925. Within one hour, three Japanese carriers were mortally damaged, afire and useless. In one hour, the American carriers with their crews and pilots had reversed the course of the naval war in the Pacific.

Even with her three sisters aflame, *Hiryu* quickly launched an attack force and followed the retreating US planes right back to their mother ships. Her crew's orders were to decimate the first American carrier they came to. That turned out to be the USS *Yorktown*, even though the Japanese had no idea it was the CV-5.

Dixie Kiefer was on the ship's bridge when first radar and then lookouts saw the approaching enemy. Men on the deck as well as those driving the ship were busy recovering the aircraft triumphantly returning from doing fatal damage to the three Japanese vessels. Every other available crewmember was at his battle station, including manning the ship's guns.

All refueling operations were promptly halted, based on the radar images, and hoses were stowed to try to avoid fire should they be hit. An 800-gallon tank of fuel on the deck was pushed overboard for the same reason. Fighter planes already in the air were sent off in the direction of the approaching enemy to deflect them.

Kiefer was not at all surprised. He fully expected a retaliatory strike if the Japanese had any planes left and a flat deck to fly off. He could tell this was not a large contingent, but it was a lethal one, very similar to what he and his crew had seen only a month earlier northeast of Australia. He quickly counted eighteen Aichi D3A dive-bombers and a half dozen or so fighter escorts. And they were coming fast, mad as hornets.

Dixie assisted his captain in sending the ship into a series of dodging zigzags, making it more difficult for the attackers to line up and dive on her. Meanwhile, deck gun crews, well experienced after the action in the Coral Sea, put up a haze of antiaircraft fire. All but five of the enemy D3As were shot down, along with half the fighters—some by *Yorktown*'s guns, some by escorts, some by the intercepting fighters.

Even so, three bombs found their way to hit the big American carrier, hard.

Once again, *Yorktown* was on fire and in danger of being wracked by more explosions and loss of life.

When the last of the surviving Japanese planes roared away, low on fuel and out of bombs, Kiefer took over assigning damage-control parties to see what was broken and what could be fixed. They were still limited in men, as many had been killed or hurt. Others had to remain at general quarters, especially at the guns, just in case there was a second wave.

Sometime during the attack, Dixie Kiefer had been struck on the right shoulder and leg by fragments that had come from an explosion of one of the bombs very near the ship's island, the structure that towers over the flight deck and serves as the ship's command center. He was knocked hard to the deck. He got back up, checked himself, and, though dizzy from the fall and some bleeding, decided he was not hurt badly

Yorktown afire after a bomb strike at Midway.

enough to need medical help. He rushed toward what appeared to be the worst of the fire.

Ignoring the pain in his shoulder and backside, Kiefer stopped along the way to retrieve a breathing apparatus from his office so he would not be overcome by the intense smoke. When he opened the door, he was almost suffocated. He pulled back, gagging and coughing. The ship's ventilation system was carrying the choking smoke throughout many of the compartments, including Dixie's office, and there was some fire inside that compartment as well. He ran on, down to the hangar deck, without the breathing mask. He would just have to make do.

Thankfully, none of the aircraft down there were on fire, nor did there appear to be any danger with the fuel hoses or storage tanks, so long as the fires that were burning could be contained. Someone had had the foresight to activate the sprinkler system, and the one plane that had caught fire had been doused. Men were busy shoving it over the side and out of the way.

But something down the way was still burning badly, sending thick, acrid smoke billowing. Then Dixie realized what it was.

Yorktown crew fights fire on the deck of their stricken ship during the Battle of Midway.

The photographic lab. The place where reconnaissance photos and film were developed. The chemicals and film stock they used in there were even more flammable than aviation gasoline.

Other crewmembers were busy elsewhere. There was nobody around. That fire had to be extinguished, or it could spread to the fuel tanks, bombs, and torpedoes. Just as he had done years before, back in Pearl, when the boat had caught fire outside his office, Dixie Kiefer took matters into his own hands.

Somehow, wading through the smoke, he found a fire hose, opened the valve, and made his way to the lab door. It was sprung open, so he moved as close as he could stand, the heat of the fire scorching his face and arms. Despite the conflagration and smoke, he was able to aim the spray at the base of the flames. Soon he had the fire knocked down and was joined by several other men who helped him put out the last of the smoky blaze.

With the fire subdued, they could assess the rest of the damage. It was not nearly as bad as expected. There was a hole in the flight deck that was quickly mended, and flight operations promptly resumed.

Firefighters get control of blazes on USS *Yorktown* during the Battle of Midway.

One of the bombs had knocked out two of the ship's nine boilers, which would soon leave them with very limited power. Despite the scalding escaping steam, crews were able to stop the leaks and restore enough power to allow the ship to make about nineteen knots, as opposed to her usual thirty-two and a half.

Another fire in the rag-stowage area deep inside the ship had broken out dangerously near more gasoline-storage tanks. But again, quick action had covered the area with CO_2 foam, and the blazes were extinguished before they could do potentially deadly damage.

One antiaircraft gun mount had been destroyed, too, killing the men who had been so bravely manning that position. Crews had picked up bodies and body parts.

Kiefer was proud of his men's efforts. They had temporarily repaired the main problems, and it had taken them just under an hour to do so. A corpsman had bandaged Dixie's shrapnel wounds; they still bled, and hurt like hell, but fortunately they appeared to be minor. And he sported a ruddy tanned look on his face from being so close to the photo lab fire.

But the blazes were out. They could still move about in the sea, even if at reduced speed. All but one gun position was ready and able. *Yorktown* was ready for whatever came next.

"Whatever" showed up just over an hour after the last attackers had disappeared into the Pacific sky, and only minutes after repairs were completed. Radar showed that the Japanese had sent a second wave off their one operating carrier. And once again, fighters were sent out from the American flat top to meet them.

Kiefer could just make out a line of aircraft, ten of them, approaching low to the horizon. This meant they were likely torpedo bombers, B5Ns, called "Kates." He could just imagine the intent looks on the pilots' faces as they hurried in to finish what their dive-bombers had failed to do.

He had no way of knowing that the Japanese were still under the impression that *Yorktown* had been sunk in the Coral Sea. Or that they had just been told that the unknown carrier the previous wave had attacked was heavily damaged, engulfed in flames (all the smoke from the lab fire), and likely sinking. This bunch was now convinced that they had happened upon yet another, different American carrier, a third flat

Crewmembers struggle to make their way on *Yorktown*'s listing deck.

top. Regardless of who she was, the B5N pilots lined up for a low-level attack, ready to launch their torpedoes at whatever ship that was flying the red, white, and blue flag.

Despite the American fighters' best efforts, the surprisingly nimble maneuvering of the big ship, and a deadly wall of fire from *Yorktown*'s guns—half the Kates were shot down—the IJN aircraft were able to hit the carrier with two torpedoes. They struck and did damage low enough on the hull that the ship quickly took on water. She quickly listed at 23 degrees and was no longer under power. She had no way to control the flooding on board. Even if they could have made power, the rudder was damaged, so they would not be able to steer.

Once again, the instant the attack seemed to be over, the exhausted damage-control teams went back to work, trying to stop flooding and see what they needed to do in order to keep the ship afloat and make her go on the desired course back home.

Meanwhile, the Japanese planes hurried back to report that they had sunk a second American aircraft carrier, leading them to assume that only one remained. Of course, both carriers "sunk" were actually *Yorktown*, and she—and her two sister carriers—all remained afloat. However, the CV-5 was listing badly and, once more, was temporarily dead in the water.

Late that afternoon, with the tilting of her deck worsening and the engineering officer reporting that without power, flooding could not be stopped, Captain Buckmaster came to an inevitable conclusion. The ship was in danger of capsizing and sinking, taking what remained of her crew down with her. He ordered all hands to the flight deck to prepare to immediately abandon ship.

It was a sad but orderly evacuation. The destroyers and cruisers in the area efficiently picked up all of the men from life rafts in the water.

Finally satisfied that everyone still alive was off the ship, Buckmaster went down a rope to a waiting raft. He, too, was picked up by a destroyer. Dixie Kiefer had reluctantly gone just ahead of his skipper.

Yorktown crew abandons ship after damage at Midway.

While all of this was happening, a scout off *Yorktown* found *Hiryu*, the lone remaining enemy carrier. Planes from *Enterprise* were rushed into the air to go and complete the job of decimating the Japanese carrier fleet. Those attackers included a squadron of dive-bombers from *Yorktown* who had been unable to land on their own ship when she was under attack and had settled down on *Enterprise* instead. At least four bombs struck *Hiryu*, and she, too, was soon ablaze. She was not able to launch or recover any more aircraft and sank the following morning.

Retribution had been completed on four of the carriers and many of the aircraft and pilots who had sucker-punched the United States at Pearl Harbor.

During the night and over the next two days, there were more attacks and counterattacks involving aircraft from the American carriers, land-based planes from Midway, and the remaining elements of the enemy fleet. More of the Japanese ships were damaged or sunk. American submarines also launched torpedoes. Even so, a sizable number of IJN warships remained afloat. All of the invasion troops were still poised on their ships, ready to go ashore and violently take the islands.

Even so, the Japanese made the decision to pull back and abandon the attempt to capture Midway. They were afraid they could not overcome the loss of their big carriers and might even sacrifice some of their battleships and other vessels to the skilled American dive-bomber pilots.

The Americans had won a huge victory. The Japanese had suffered a terrible loss. More than three thousand IJN personnel had died, including several ship captains and second-in-command officers who chose to go down with their vessels rather than live to fight again someday.

The next morning, from his perch on a rescue ship, Captain Buckmaster was amazed to see that *Yorktown* had not sunk during the night after all. The vessel was still afloat. Not only had the angle of her slanting decks stopped increasing, but she was also a degree or two closer to being level. There might actually be a chance she could be reclaimed rather than allowed to sink. With the task force commander's approval, Buckmaster made the decision to send a salvage crew back aboard the ship. They were told to do what they could to stabilize her and make her more seaworthy in preparation for being pulled back to Pearl Harbor for repairs.

Yorktown, assumed sinking, guarded by destroyer USS *Balch* (DD-363).

Yorktown was soon under tow by USS *Vireo* (AT-144), a former minesweeper now repurposed as a sea tugboat. Several destroyers had been arrayed around her, shielding her from attack. That included USS *Hammann* (DD-412), which pulled close enough that the carrier could be hooked up to the destroyer to supply auxiliary power, primarily for the flood pumps.

Yorktown's new onboard salvage crew consisted of 29 officers—including Dixie Kiefer, who commanded the party—and 141 sailors. The volunteer salvage crew went to work under the supervision of their XO, mostly pushing damaged aircraft and equipment over the side and cutting away the bombed-out gun position. This was done in an effort to reduce weight topside and allow the ship to be more stable. In addition, they pumped out flooded compartments to try to stay ahead of the inrushing seawater and keep the carrier upright.

They also had another job—a grisly one. They had to put the bodies of their deceased shipmates into bags and give them a proper sea burial. First, though, they had to place the identification tags and papers of the killed-in-action into a big, brown bag so families could be properly notified.

The work was backbreaking, uncomfortable, and dangerous. But they were quickly making progress, getting the big vessel shipshape and on her way back to where she could be repaired to fight another day.

Then, just before sunset on June 6, a Japanese submarine slipped between protective destroyers. The I-boat launched three torpedoes at the wounded flat top. Two of them hit the big ship hard. The third struck *Hammann* amidships, cutting her in two. She sank immediately. Eight men died.

This time the carrier had definitely suffered fatal wounds. She was most certainly sinking, doing so rapidly, in imminent danger of capsizing. Many of the men aboard the carrier had been knocked down brutally by the blasts of the torpedoes. Several were sent reeling overboard, into the sea. There were more injuries, some of them serious. The decision once again came down to abandon the ship, and to do so immediately. Not only was *Yorktown* now sinking fast, but the I-boat might also still be in the area. Or another one just like it.

At that moment, Dixie Kiefer's job changed. He was now in charge of evacuating the remaining crewmen—the ones who were not killed in the torpedo blast—from the ship. It would not be easy. Especially getting the men who had been hurt onto stretchers and over the side. And doing so in one hell of a hurry, before the carrier sank and sucked them all down with her.

Kiefer stood at the edge of the deck watching his men as they grabbed ropes and slid down into the water. Life rafts waited for them. The other destroyers were maneuvering to be able to pick them up.

He also discovered, to his dismay, that the bag of ID tags of the deceased men had been lost in the torpedo attack. There was nothing he could do about it.

Then Dixie heard shouts for help. A wounded sailor was in trouble. The rope being used to lower his stretcher had gotten tangled. The young man was about to be dumped into the sea. In his condition and from that height, there would be little chance he could survive such a fall.

Kiefer ran over and grabbed hold of the rope himself, righting the stretcher. It took all the strength he could muster. Then, with an encouraging word for the hurt sailor, the XO began deliberately lowering him down toward the sea.

The rope suddenly slipped through his hands, badly burning both of Kiefer's palms and the pads of his fingers. Even so, he kept as much of a grip as he could manage, easing somewhat the wounded boy's landing in the water below.

There was no corpsman available to treat Dixie's hands—no easy way to get a painkiller shot or soothing salve. He simply spat on the seared flesh, looked over the side to make sure somebody had pulled the wounded sailor from the water, and then continued doing what he had been doing: making certain every man got over the side and was making it into a life raft. The *Vireo*, the ship that had been towing them, had cut her lines by then and joined the other ships that were picking up men who were in rafts or floating in the sea.

With the last surviving crewman off the ship, it was Dixie's turn to go over the side. He took a deep breath, grabbed a rope, gritted his teeth, and attempted to ignore the awful pain in his hands when he tried to grip the line. Then he started lowering himself down to the water below.

Halfway, with his burned palms screaming, he could no longer support his considerable weight, the heft all those flight physicals had fussed about over the years.

He fell.

It was a long way down. Even so, landing in the sea did not cause further injury. During the plunge, though—a drop Kiefer later estimated to be about fifty feet—his right leg struck the heavy metal armor belt that circled the hull of the carrier near the waterline. He knew at once that he had broken bones, either in the ankle or in the foot.

Lord knows, by then Dixie Kiefer recognized what a broken bone felt like!

He struggled to the surface, gasping for air. The pain from the salty seawater on his hands and radiating from his newly broken bones was almost too much to bear. The shrapnel wounds stung, too.

Luckily, he spotted a life raft nearby. He swam for it, still coughing and gasping, as much from the agonizing pain as from the water he had swallowed at the rough conclusion of his fall.

But when he got to the raft, he could tell that the men inside were all badly wounded. Nobody was able to row in the direction of a ship that could pull them from the shark-infested waters.

Kiefer did all he could do. Despite the agony from his injuries, he ducked down and began to swim as best he could, using his forehead and shoulder to shove the raft along. He cupped his scorched hands, grabbing water, kicking with his badly fractured ankle and foot, trying to push the raft toward the rescue ship.

Somehow, they made progress. Slow, agonizing progress.

"Sir, you okay?" one of the men inside the raft asked Kiefer. "You don't sound so good."

"Aw, I'm . . . I'm all right, son. I got to make sure . . . make sure you boys get pulled in . . . before we drift off to Alaska or somewhere . . . or a hungry shark comes along . . ."

Soon Dixie was completely exhausted, unable to push anymore. A couple of the injured men in the raft realized the officer was bushed, in

Yorktown finally sinks during the Battle of Midway.

danger of slipping beneath the waves. They ignored their own pain then and were finally able to struggle and pull Kiefer into the raft.

They were all rescued by a destroyer crew shortly thereafter. The wounded men had a story to tell, too—about how their ship's XO had fought through his own injuries to help make sure the sailors in the raft got picked up.

The Battle of Midway was a turning point in the war in the Pacific. Certainly there would be years of fighting yet to go, but the Japanese carriers that were lost over those two days would prove to be a big problem for the Imperial Japanese Navy. The enemy's navy was no longer invincible, nor were they able to dominate in the new-style carrier war.

More than three thousand Japanese died in the battle, with more than two thousand of them killed on those four aircraft carriers. Just over three hundred Americans died. Almost half of those were men and officers from USS *Yorktown*.

The Japanese people did not hear of the crushing defeat at Midway. The showdown was declared a glorious victory for the Imperial Navy, one in which three American aircraft carriers were gloriously sunk. Never mind that all three of those were the *Yorktown*.

Midway remained in Allied hands and became a crucial submarine base. Subs from there went on to wreak havoc in the shipping lanes the Japanese tried to use to import those valuable resources, the pursuit of which had led to their original plan to expand their empire.

Dixie Kiefer went back to Hawaii to begin to mend. His leg was put into a plaster cast, and he was transferred to the stateside naval hospital at Mare Island, California, for more treatment. He was officially declared "unfit for duty for an indefinite period of time."

Dixie was out of the war for a bit. However, the navy would eventually put him back to work, even as he recovered from his bum foot and ankle and his blistered hands. Initially, his job would be a long way from any ocean—but not far at all from where he spent much of his boyhood.

Meanwhile, in the autumn of 1942, he learned that he was to receive the Navy Cross—the US Navy's second-highest honor for valor in combat, just behind the Medal of Honor—for his actions at Midway. The citation for the award reads, in its entirety:

The President of the United States of America takes pleasure in presenting the Navy Cross to Commander Dixie Kiefer, United States Navy, for extraordinary heroism and distinguished service in the line of his profession as Executive Officer of the Aircraft Carrier U.S.S. YORKTOWN (CV-5), in preparation for, during and after action against enemy Japanese forces in the Battle of Midway, on 4 June 1942. Through sound judgment, thorough planning and exceptional courage, Commander Kiefer contributed greatly toward the high state of readiness for battle which made it possible for the YORKTOWN to face the powerful bombing and torpedo attacks of the enemy with aggressive fighting spirit and enabled her Air Group to accomplish their hazardous missions with inspired efficiency. When the stricken vessel was being gutted by raging fires, he, being unable to obtain a rescue breathing apparatus from his own smoke-filled cabin, entered the photographic laboratory, which was a flaming inferno from burning films, and conducted the first fire-fighting there. Later, while directing the abandonment of the YORKTOWN, Commander Kiefer, in lowering an injured man into a life raft, burned his hands so severely that when he himself went over the side and descended the line, he was unable to support his own weight. In the resultant fall he struck the ship's armor belt and suffered a compound fracture of the foot and ankle. Despite acute pain, he gallantly swam alongside of and pushed a life raft toward a rescuing destroyer until he became so completely exhausted he had to be pulled out of the water. His courageous initiative and unselfish devotion to duty were in keeping with the highest traditions of the United States Naval Service.

Dixie Kiefer was now a bona fide war hero.

CHAPTER NINE

Shore Duty, Movie Acting, and First Command

As it turned out, Dixie Kiefer was "unfit for duty" because of his injuries at Midway until the end of January 1943. Being laid up for seven months was certainly frustrating for him. He knew how much the US Navy and his country needed a man with his experience out there fighting a vicious and fanatical enemy. It was small consolation that the navy promoted him to the rank of captain two weeks before he was dismissed from the hospital.

It did make him feel better when he learned that while he continued to get back on his feet—literally—he would be put to use doing something he knew well: helping to train new pilots. And eventually doing it in a part of the country with which he was also familiar, the middle portion, once again far from the ocean.

He was named commander of the Naval Aviation Station in Olathe, Kansas, near Kansas City, and only about two hundred miles from his boyhood home in Lincoln, Nebraska. He was to start that job immediately upon getting clearance from the navy docs and leaving the hospital in Mare Island. He was soon doing double duty, at least for a couple of months, heading up the Naval Academy's Aviation Department in Annapolis as well. Then, in July 1943, he became chief of staff of the Naval Air Primary Training facility in Kansas City, serving there until April 1944.

The navy never had reason to doubt Dixie Kiefer's abilities when it came to commanding men or running a ship. So once they were convinced he was once again physically able to handle the job, they gave him a bunch of men on a mighty big vessel. In February 1944, he received orders to report to Newport News Shipbuilding and Drydock Company, his new duty starting on April 8. There, the finishing touches were being put on the new USS *Ticonderoga* (CV-14), an *Essex*-class aircraft carrier. Dixie Kiefer was to be her first skipper. And an old friend and shipmate, Bill Burch, the hero pilot from Kiefer's days on *Yorktown*, was to be his XO. Burch had been considered as a PCO— prospective commanding officer—for the new vessel, but his old shipmate Dixie Kiefer got the job.

The big ship was named for Fort Ticonderoga, an eighteenth-century stronghold that played a major role in both the French and Indian War and the Revolutionary War. It is located in what is today upstate New York, on the southern end of Lake Champlain.

USS *Ticonderoga* (CV-14).

We should note here that the fort for which Dixie Kiefer's aircraft carrier was named is only about two hundred miles north of and in the same general range of mountains as Mount Beacon, New York, the crag that will play a key part later in this story. However, it was originally the Hancock *to which he was to report for command, not the* Ticonderoga. *This is yet another in the long list of coincidences and quirks that run throughout this tale.*

Construction had started officially on the vessel in Norfolk on February 1, 1943, just as Kiefer was reporting to Olathe. The ship under construction was at that point named *Hancock*. That changed three months later. She had her name swapped with another carrier that was then being built as *Ticonderoga* CV-19 at Bethlehem Steel in Quincy, Massachusetts.

There was a very practical reason for the name switch: money. The John Hancock Insurance Company agreed to conduct a bond drive to help pay for the ship being built in the corporation's home state if it would carry the *Hancock* name instead of the one coming together down in Virginia. The navy readily agreed.

The Norfolk-built carrier was formally launched on February 7, 1944, as its new captain-to-be was still serving in Kansas, waiting to report and oversee final construction and sea trials and to prepare her for commissioning. No one could have known at the time that although Kiefer would only serve as the ship's captain for about a year—an action-packed year, by the way—the big vessel he would help prepare for war would ultimately be in service to the United States for almost thirty years, until September 1973.

Though she was being built as an *Essex*-class carrier, *Ticonderoga* had a few key design modifications, based on the hard-won experience of the other flat tops seeing action in the real world. She could also include changes that were forbidden by former treaties that went away when the war started. The major difference was that she was sixteen to eighteen feet longer than her predecessors. That was primarily to allow for mounting antiaircraft guns on her bow. Because of this and other alterations, future vessels in the series with similar features were considered *Ticonderoga*-class vessels and were sometimes referred to as "long bow" models. She continued to be modified over the years, so "The Big T" (as she quickly became known) graduated to be a *Hancock*-class ship by the end of her career.

She was one large lady. As built, she displaced 27,100 tons and was 888 feet from bow to stern. That was more than 60 feet longer than the late *Yorktown* had been. She was powered by eight boilers that spun four massive Westinghouse steam turbines. She could make thirty-three knots. The elevators that lifted planes from the hangar deck up to the flight deck and back down were the size of tennis courts.

Ticonderoga's crew count would eventually swell to almost 3,500 officers and enlisted men.

When commissioned, she was armed with four twin five-inch guns, four single five-inch guns, eight quadruple forty-millimeter guns, and forty-six single twenty-millimeter cannons. Practically all this weaponry was intended for antiaircraft use. She was able to carry and operate between ninety and one hundred aircraft of various types. The Big T was one formidable warship.

A young sailor named Edward Kelly received his orders to report to the new *Ticonderoga* in January 1944. When he showed up as ordered, he reported to a chief, since there were not yet any officers assigned to the vessel. And since the ship was still under construction and the navy preferred that crewmembers not get in the way of shipyard workers, they pretty much had nothing to do.

The chief told Kelly, "Our fence is not but three feet high. There is an open gate every fifty feet. You keep your own liberty card. We'll let you know any time there is a morning muster or any other reason for you to show up here. Have a good time."

So that was exactly what Kelly and his shipmates—many already buddies from serving together on his previous ship—set out to do. They were sitting in a bar one morning at about 10:00 a.m., enjoying a beer breakfast, when an officer walked in the door. He headed over to the sailors' table and the men braced themselves for some flack.

However, the guy grinned and winked.

"You boys off the *Ticonderoga?*" he asked. They confirmed they were. "Well, it is a pleasure to meet you. I'm Dixie Kiefer, your new skipper."

The sailors did not know how to react or whether they were now in big trouble. They need not have worried.

"They issued me a jeep while we're here," Kiefer said, "and I'm staying out near your barracks. If you ever need a ride, just flag me down and I'll give you a lift."

Kelly and the other young sailors knew immediately that they liked their captain.

"Have a good time, men. We'll get to serious work soon enough."

Offering rides to his men was a hallmark of Dixie Kiefer's command style. It was just another way he could show his appreciation to his men and allowed him to get to know them, their families, where they were from, and what they were thinking.

Between Midway and the *Ticonderoga*, Kiefer took time for an interesting side job while he recuperated. The US Navy and the motion picture studio 20th Century Fox were working on a documentary film about aircraft carriers and the effect they were having on the war. Using actual combat footage—much of it taken by gun cameras on aircraft during real action—as well as more film specifically shot for the movie aboard *Yorktown*, *The Fighting Lady* detailed the story of a carrier believed to have been modeled on the USS *Yorktown* (the newer CV-10). Dixie was asked to play a minor role as the ship's captain, a man named "Dixie." He is shown speaking to his crew as he assumes command, using the ship's announcement system, telling them his intention was to go all the way to Japan, knowing they would have to fight all the way there, and then to drop the carrier's anchor at Yokohama. And when that happened, he intended to throw a party and everyone was invited. The crewmen on deck cheer wildly in response. It was typecasting at its best!

Not only did the movie serve its intended purpose of building up patriotic fervor, but *The Fighting Lady* also won the Academy Award for "Best Documentary Feature" of 1944. Now Dixie Kiefer was even more than a war hero—he was a major part of an Oscar-winning motion picture.

Though she was commissioned in early May 1944, *Ticonderoga* did not get under way until June 26, spending the two months still in Norfolk, continuing to get ready and to collect the aircraft she would haul. Those planes were dubbed Air Group 80. Then she and her crew were sent down to the area near Trinidad for a two-week shakedown cruise. And that gave them the opportunity to do something of which Dixie Kiefer wholeheartedly approved.

He wanted a chance to drive his men hard, putting his ship's crew and the flight crews through every possible scenario they might encounter once they were in the Pacific. He would demand perfection in drills, but he also wanted them to relax, to bond during their off time. More than anything, Kiefer wanted to meld his ship into one solid, dependable battle unit, a group that not only wanted to fight the enemy but also was well trained in how to do it in what Kiefer knew would be the most effective way. Those fifteen days in the Caribbean gave him his best opportunity to effectively impart his own hard-won knowledge to his officers, sailors, and fliers. To show them that their skipper was one of them, understood their jobs as well as they did, and was willing to roll up his sleeves and go to work if that was what it took to strike a blow against the enemy. Any future experience would be gained in the heat and turmoil of battle.

It was during this time that Kiefer, standing on the bridge, addressed the crew on the ship's announcement system. They all stood before him, aligned along the vessel's massive flight deck.

"Men, I just wanted to remind you of where I am planning on going," he said in his pronounced Midwestern twang. "I'm planning on going all the way to Tokyo Bay!" There were hearty cheers from all. "And I intend to drop Big T's 'hook' at Yokohama!"

This time Kiefer was certain they could have heard his crew's lusty reaction all the way to Venezuela.

After a quick run back to Norfolk and then back down for passage through the Panama Canal—giving Dixie the opportunity to once again tell his tale of being hit by a flying aircraft years before while there—*Ticonderoga* turned northwest to arrive at San Diego in mid-September. The squeeze through the Canal was an adventure. The big carrier barely fit in some of the waterway's locks—ropes were used as bumpers—but she made it with no scrapes or scratches.

The carrier took on more aircraft and pilots in San Diego, loaded up with fuel and provisions, and then soon steamed away for Hawaii. There was time out there in the middle of the Pacific for more training and work, mostly spent perfecting procedures for transferring bombs from transport ships to aircraft carriers while under way, and accomplishing that feat without blowing up either vessel.

Then, finally, Big T was under way again, this time bound for the western Pacific, to Ulithi in the Caroline Islands, to join up with Task Force 38, part of Admiral William "Bull" Halsey's Third Fleet, and the new aircraft carrier's initial introduction to war.

There was a general feeling among many that the end of World War II was inevitable and imminent. Those fighting in the Pacific knew better. Such bloody clashes as Iwo Jima, the Philippines, and Okinawa still lay ahead. An enemy as determined as Japan would, as many knew, fight until the very end, to the last man. Only a handful knew of the work on the atomic bomb. Plans were well under way for an eventual invasion of the Japanese Home Islands. Estimates of potential casualties on both sides in such an operation were staggering.

The best hope of the Allies was to sink every warship and shoot down every airplane the enemy had. Cut supply lines and shipping lanes. Starve the Home Islands. Block natural resources necessary to wage war. Capture each tiny island—at a high human price—up the chain to Japan. Then launch a D-Day-type invasion.

Dixie Kiefer, of all people, knew exactly what to expect when his new ship ultimately joined the war. So did the more experienced men in his crew and flight team. The others were certainly about to find out. They had not yet witnessed the single-mindedness of the Japanese pilots or the tenacity of their submarines.

Captain Kiefer could only hope that all the training they had done for the past four months had sunk in—that they were, to a man, ready. Hope that his constant preaching and cheering on had the men primed for the most vicious battling imaginable.

He was well aware that the Japanese were, by the winter of 1944, becoming even more desperate. They were now willing to do anything to stop Allied troops, aircraft, and ships.

Anything, including deliberately crashing their airplanes, heavily loaded with explosives, into targets.

Captain Dixie Kiefer in full combat dress on the bridge of "Big T."

CHAPTER TEN

"Divine Wind"

As EXPECTED, *TICONDEROGA* SAW ACTION QUICKLY. INTENSE ACTION. And Dixie Kiefer was delighted with how his crew performed. That team-building effort in the Caribbean had apparently paid off.

The first week of November 1944, Big T joined the other carriers in Task Force 38 as they provided air cover for the ground forces involved in the Battle of Leyte. This was part of General Douglas MacArthur's promise to return to the Philippines after he and his staff had been chased away from that country at the start of the war. *Ticonderoga* launched her first air strike on the morning of November 5. Her airplanes spent the next two days bashing enemy ships near the main Philippine island of Luzon, as well as land-based airfields there. Some of her planes helped sink a heavy Japanese cruiser and shot down six Japanese aircraft while damaging two dozen others.

Later that day, the men on *Ticonderoga* got their first look at the latest and most terrifying enemy tactic—kamikaze aircraft. Just after 4:00 p.m., the Japanese attacked the carriers with a group of the suicide planes. Two of them somehow got through the wall of antiaircraft fire and crashed into the carrier USS *Lexington*—CV-16, a newer ship named for *Yorktown's* old mate that had been lost in the Coral Sea—which was steaming not far from Big T at the time.

Fire instantly erupted up and down *Lexington's* decks, almost engulfing the carrier's island. It looked dire, but damage-control teams sprang to action and had the fire extinguished within twenty minutes. The carrier continued normal operations just in time for her gun crews to shoot down another suicide plane, this one headed directly for *Ticonderoga*. Tokyo Rose would later tell shortwave listeners worldwide that *Lexington* had been sunk even though she had suffered what were only considered minor casualties and limited damage.

The next day, *Ticonderoga* launched two fighter sweeps and two bombing strikes against the Luzon airfields, along with other enemy shipping in the vicinity. Her airmen returned later that day claiming the obliteration of thirty-five enemy aircraft and damaging attacks on six Japanese ships in Manila Bay.

Dixie Kiefer was once again thrilled with his ship's performance. Though he continued to compile a long list of improvements and adjustments he wanted to make as quickly as possible, he took time to go up and down the decks personally congratulating and thanking every man he met for the jobs they had done. At his suggestion, everyone referred to him as "Captain Dixie." His reputation as a sailor's skipper continued

Ticonderoga crewmembers are briefed before action in Manila Bay.

to grow. Some of the more regimented among the ship's officers were not quite so enamored of Kiefer's familiar leadership style and relaxed demeanor with the enlisted crew, but Dixie did not mind. He firmly believed that every man would be more willing to do his best and lay his life on the line for a captain who recognized the importance of every crewmember, not just the officers and flight teams.

With the congratulating done, though, the primary subject he wanted to discuss with his wardroom and fighter pilots was the kamikaze attacks. Now that he had seen firsthand the deadly determination of the Japanese pilots, he was more convinced than ever of the threat they presented to his ship and its men.

Even a single suicide pilot, finding the right spot on which to crash and doing so at the perfect time—when aircraft were being fueled and loaded with bombs, torpedoes, and ammunition—could put even a ship as big as an aircraft carrier on the bottom. And they could claim hundreds, maybe thousands, of lives in the process. It had happened already, back in October, when a single suicide dive-bomber had struck the small escort carrier USS *St. Lo* (CVE-63), setting off a fire that caused the ship's torpedo and bomb magazine—the ammunition storage area—to explode. She sank within thirty minutes, taking the lives of 143 men.

After recovering the last of the aircraft, Kiefer issued the order to head eastward to meet up with an oiler and supply vessel, to refuel ship and aircraft and resupply the carrier, and to prepare for the next action. Even so, the primary thought on the captain's mind was the suicide attacks and how to try to minimize their effects, both physical and psychological.

Kamikaze is the Japanese word for "divine wind" or "spirit wind." While all Japanese soldiers, sailors, and pilots were supposed to be willing to die without question or hesitation for their emperor and Empire, the suicide fliers were specifically detailed to do just that. Almost four thousand Japanese kamikaze pilots died in World War II, either shot down before they could do their damage or among the estimated 20 percent who successfully hit a target. Even though such a tactic was born out of desperation, and though none of the Allies thought it had any chance of turning the course of the war, it was still something to be studied, to find a way to minimize its consequences.

Aircraft, typically the famous Zeros, were specially prepared as human-directed missiles, heavily loaded with explosives, bombs, or fuel in order to do the maximum amount of damage. The Zero could fly at over 300 miles per hour—even faster when diving on a target with no intention of pulling up and away—and had a range of almost two thousand miles. Other planes—in effect, more like piloted bombs than aircraft—even featured landing gear that could be jettisoned just after take-off and reused. The airplane would have no need for wheels once it was airborne, and, at least to the Japanese, the pilot was expendable, whereas the landing gear was not.

The kamikaze pilot's training manual, later found in cockpits of aircraft, made it clear that the men had a sacred mission: "Transcend life and death. When you eliminate all thoughts about life and death, you will be able to totally disregard your earthly life. This will also enable you to concentrate your attention on eradicating the enemy with unwavering determination, meanwhile reinforcing your excellence in flight skills."

There was no lack of volunteers for such one-way missions. Three times as many men sought to take suicide flights as they had planes for them to fly. In most cases, experienced pilots were rejected. They were required to train the younger men on how to wedge themselves between bombs and other explosives and fly the piloted missiles to their deaths.

Beginning in October 1944 and first employed in the Leyte Gulf, the suicide tactics quickly improved the effectiveness of the Japanese air attacks, but at the cost of still more of their dwindling supply of trained pilots and battle-ready aircraft. Even so, the Imperial Japanese Navy was frantic enough following a series of terrible defeats that they felt they had no other choice but to send skilled fliers to certain death in order to try to repel the Allied naval efforts.

Not only was the method more effective from an accuracy stand-point, but it was also a strong emotional weapon. Gun crews on ships were stunned by how the suicide pilots were able to ignore the curtain of antiaircraft fire they threw up and somehow find their way to the ships they were targeting. Fighter pilots, flying cover for targeted ships, also had little success in trying to chase away the kamikazes.

Japanese kamikaze pilots play with a puppy.

"Relentless" was too mild a word to describe the hell-bent fliers. And that wild-eyed willingness to deliberately complete a fiery crash onto a ship's deck was terrifying to even the most courageous sailor. How do you deter an attacker who is perfectly willing to die? What could warships possibly do to minimize the damage these resolute attackers might inflict?

Captain Dixie presents a cake to one of his pilots commemorating Big T's six thousandth aircraft landing.

That question was precisely what Kiefer wanted to discuss with his other officers and members of the task force. They had been lucky this most recent outing. *Lexington* had recovered from her own brush with a kamikaze just in time to save Big T's bacon.

The truth was that nobody had any answers. The best hope was for the ships' gun crews to shoot down the attackers before they had a chance to crash. Or for fighters flying cover to chase them through the air, attempting to shoot them down before they completed their death mission. At the same time, they hoped the fighter pilots would keep the kamikazes from lining up for a well-placed strike. But that was easier said than done.

The only other thing to do was to be ready should a kamikaze attack come and to recover should one or more hit home. Complete refueling and rearming as efficiently as possible. Drain gas hoses immediately after use. Have sprinkler systems ready to employ. Be ready to fight fire; tend to wounded crewmen; salvage what equipment, machinery, and weapons could be put back into service; and keep the vital ship in the fight. Especially the carriers, the vessels the suicide fliers preferred to target. Once launched, aircraft had to have a place to land before they ran out of fuel.

For the rest of November and into December, *Ticonderoga* and her mates in Task Force 38 continued to take a heavy toll on enemy shipping and land-based facilities in the Philippines. But despite the success of her flight crews and gunners, there were some close calls. On November 25, the Sunday after Thanksgiving, a kamikaze plane struck sister carrier USS *Essex*, which was operating within sight of Big T.

The Zero hit the port edge of the *Essex* flight deck just as planes were being gassed up for takeoff. There was extensive damage. Fifteen men died instantly, and another forty-four were wounded. But it could have been worse.

When a second suicide aircraft zoomed in to attack the stricken carrier, *Ticonderoga*'s gunners joined those firing from other ships in the area, just as *Lexington* had done earlier to protect Big T. They shot the Zero down before it could line up and do more damage—maybe fatal—to the already blazing *Essex*. That afternoon, while damage-control parties worked to get *Essex* and her flight deck back to operational again, *Ticonderoga* busily recovered aircrew that the wounded carrier was unable to receive.

Kiefer and the crew of *Ticonderoga* continued to work hard and kick butt in support of the retaking of the Philippines. Dixie would later receive the Silver Star medal, the country's third-highest award for valor in combat, in part for his leadership as captain of the big carrier in the Philippines campaign.

The citation for the award declares it was being given to Kiefer "for conspicuous gallantry and intrepidity as Commanding Officer of the U.S.S. TICONDEROGA in action against enemy Japanese forces in the Philippine Islands . . . from October 29, 1944 . . . a skillful seaman, Commodore [then Captain] Kiefer maneuvered his ship to the best tactical advantage during attacks on enemy aircraft, shipping and installations and, by his excellent leadership, directed his air detachment in carrying out attacks which resulted in the sinking of thirty-two enemy vessels and the probable sinking of eighty-two others, the destruction of one hundred thirty-seven hostile planes and the probable destruction of eighty-six others."

Kiefer, of course, gave all credit to his officers and sailors and flight crews. As they pulled away from their station in mid-December to seek fuel, "medicinal" alcohol was once again dispensed, tall tales were told, backs were slapped, and, despite the loss of a minimal number of pilots, the mood was sky-high aboard Big T.

They had done their jobs well, helping to cripple the enemy, effectively breaking the back of the Imperial Japanese Navy. Though enemy troops fighting in the Philippines would not officially surrender until after the war ended, the invasion by Allied troops was well under way by Christmas 1944, and despite continued fighting, the country would soon be under US control.

The Allies were also making progress with their efforts to overcome the kamikaze attacks. Using superior radar, far-ranging fighters were dispatched to seek out and shoot down suicide squadrons long before they could reach groups of Allied warships. Intelligence determined which airfields were primarily being used to launch the kamikazes, and they were pounded mercilessly in an attempt to take out planes and pilots and to render runways useless. Cover aircraft also began to fly over task forces twenty-four/seven, effectively keeping a protective ceiling over warships.

Even so, the Japanese remained committed to about the only hope they had to cripple the US Navy fighting vessels. And though the new defenses seemed to help, the strong-minded suicide pilots continued to be willing to die for their emperor and their ancestors. From October 25, 1944, to January 25, 1945, kamikazes sank two escort carriers and three destroyers. They also damaged twenty-three carriers, five battleships, nine cruisers, twenty-three destroyers, and twenty-seven vessels of other types. In those suicide attacks, 738 Americans were killed, and another 1,300 were wounded.

There is no way to quantify the effect the kamikazes had on morale.

Even so, as Captain Dixie and *Ticonderoga* steamed around on December 16, there was suddenly a bigger concern. The seas were growing noticeably rougher. Too rough to attempt to refuel from one of the big tankers waiting for them and the other members of Task Force 38. They simply had to find calmer waters. Otherwise, an already-dicey refueling operation would become dangerous, almost impossible. And a carrier without fuel for its boilers or its airplane engines was of little use.

If they did not have better weather soon, they would all have to head back to Ulithi in the Caroline Islands. Many of the smaller ships in the task force already were running too low on fuel to be able to make that trip.

By nightfall on December 16, weather conditions had grown worse still. By then, TF-38 consisted of seven fleet carriers, six light carriers, eight battleships, fifteen cruisers, and about four dozen destroyers. Admiral Halsey sent word that all ships should prepare for a blow, but forecasters did not expect anything that would require them to leave the area or otherwise alter their plans. He based this assessment on predictions from Pearl Harbor, even though weather observers within the fleet were considerably more concerned. The forecast was for more rough weather, but nothing to really be concerned about. A minor typhoon of little consequence, and it would move northward, passing hundreds of miles away from the fleet. It would likely blow itself out. Then they would be able to quench the thirst of all those vessels and get them back into the war.

An old salt like Dixie Kiefer knew better. He relied on intuition and the aching in all those previously broken bones to tell him what this particular "divine wind" might actually do. He took steps to rig his ship for a major storm and vowed to change course as necessary to ride it out.

Exactly as Kiefer suspected, Mother Nature was about to throw a real punch. It would prove to be a blow to the chin of the Allied fleet that the Japanese could only wish they still had the strength to land.

CHAPTER ELEVEN

Halsey's Typhoons

IN THE LATE THIRTEENTH CENTURY, KUBLAI KHAN, WITH THE INTENtion of capturing Japan, sent his Mongol army of 40,000 men eastward aboard an estimated 1,000 vessels. On the evening before the invasion, a sudden hurricane hit, killing 13,000 men and sending the Mongols fleeing. Seven years later, the army once again approached Japan, this time in a massive fleet of 4,500 ships with more than 145,000 men. After an initial skirmish, the victorious Mongols returned to their ships to rest for the night and prepare for the final glorious assault. But once again, another typhoon struck. Even more powerful than the previous one, this storm drowned 100,000 invaders. Kublai Khan once again recalled his army and would never again attempt to invade Japan.

The Japanese poetically referred to the two fortuitous typhoons as *kamikaze*, or "divine wind." And that was the origin of the name later given to suicide pilots during the last desperate year of World War II.

One week before Christmas 1944, Japan would once again have the benefit of what it saw as divine intervention against a would-be conqueror. Admiral William "Bull" Halsey had his Task Force 38—including USS *Ticonderoga*—in the midst of refueling efforts, preparing to continue its support of the invasion of the Philippines. At least that was what they were attempting to do when the seas grew uncommonly rough and a storm showed up on the fleet's radar screens. The experts back in Pearl Harbor had badly misread the typhoon. That included the possibilities of the typhoon growing stronger, as well as the path it would likely take.

Based on that errant information, Halsey sent his ships sailing right into the teeth of what would officially be dubbed Typhoon Cobra. Hundred-foot swells and wind gusts greater than 140 miles per hour soon had the fleet scattered over 3,000 square miles of ocean. By the time hurricane warnings were finally radioed to the ships, three destroyers had been lost: USS *Spence* (DD-512), with 317 men killed and 23 eventually rescued; USS *Hull* (DD-350), with 202 men drowned and 62 survivors; and USS *Monaghan* (DD-354), with 256 men lost and only 6 survivors. In the case of two of the destroyers, they were so low on fuel that they were top-heavy. Suffering rolls as severe as 70 degrees, seawater went down their stacks, disabling their engines. Without power, they were no match

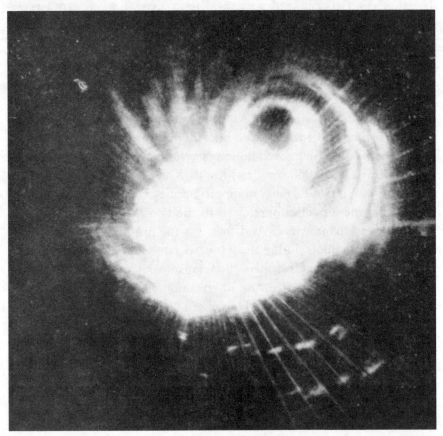

Rare radar image of Typhoon Cobra, December 1944.

for the deadly seas and wind. Other destroyers, once they were aware of the severity of the storm they faced, promptly pumped seawater into their fuel tanks, giving them just enough stability to avoid a similar fate.

One of the six *Monaghan* survivors, Joseph McCrane, told his rescuers a harrowing tale.

"The storm broke in all its fury," he reported. "We started to roll, heaving to the starboard, and everyone was holding on to something and praying as hard as he could. We knew that we had lost our power and were dead in the water. We must have taken about seven or eight rolls to the starboard before she went over on her side."

Once in the water, things were even worse. Some survivors had managed to grab some provisions before the ship flipped over.

"Every time we opened a can of Spam, more sharks would appear," McCrane related. "Toward evening, some of the boys began to crack under the strain. The second night most of the fellows had really lost their heads, believing they had seen land and houses."

Of course, there was nothing out there but towering waves and the occasional shark fin—until two days later, when the half-dozen men were finally rescued.

Ticonderoga's sister flat top, the light carrier USS *Monterey* (CVL-26), found herself in dire trouble when gale and waves tore aircraft loose on her hangar deck. A fire erupted, threatening the ship and her crew. Admiral Halsey sent word to abandon the ship and ordered other vessels in the area to attempt to recover crewmembers in the roiling waters. The ship's skipper, though, relayed back a message: "We can fix this." He sent one of his officers, the general quarters officer of the deck, down below to assess the situation and make recommendations.

That young officer was Lieutenant Gerald Ford, the future US senator, vice president, and president. Ford was almost washed overboard in the process, but he reported back that the crew was already making progress against the fire, despite rolls of greater than 20 degrees. At times, it appeared the ship would capsize. Ford joined in and helped to save the *Monterey*. Three men would die in the effort.

Another sister light carrier, the USS *Cowpens* (CVL-25), had a similar problem. A Hellcat fighter broke loose from its triple lashing

Light carrier USS *Cowpens* (CVL-25) almost capsizes during Typhoon Cobra.

and struck a catwalk. There was immediately gasoline-fed fire everywhere. Then a bomb-handling truck rolled across the deck and struck another fighter plane. Even so, and in the midst of the raging storm, the men of *Cowpens* fought the fires and eventually controlled them. One sailor was lost.

Meanwhile, over on Big T, Dixie Kiefer suspected that weather forecasters had miscalculated. Even if they had not, he instinctively knew there was a possibility the storm could grow stronger than predicted and its path in that part of the world could be erratic and changeable. He prepared his ship, crew, and aircraft for the worst and picked his own direction in which to sail, bringing his escorts with him. He chose to tactfully disregard Admiral Halsey's orders to steam right into what turned out to be a major typhoon.

Unlike the reports from other vessels in the path of the storm, *Ticonderoga*'s logs show no panic or individual heroic efforts. It was business as usual. Even in the worst of the storm, they continued to watch for Japanese attackers—especially the startlingly swift and sneaky kamikazes—and kept on the ready the carrier's complement of airplanes and pilots, just in case there was a break in the clouds and they needed to fly. Everyone did his job calmly and efficiently.

There was some minor damage to *Ticonderoga*, the most serious to the ship's radar antenna. But with the early preparation and course correction, the brave work of the crew, and the skill of her captain and other officers, aided by the sheer size and seaworthiness of Big T, they came through the massive blow just fine.

Though certainly not as bad as the carnage that befell the Mongols back in the 1200s, the final damage reports were sobering. Admiral Chester Nimitz, the navy's commander for the "Pacific Areas," later declared that the typhoon's impact "represented a more crippling blow to the Third Fleet than it might be expected to suffer in anything less than a major action."

The sunken destroyers and men lost were the worst of it. But in addition, nine other ships, including one light cruiser, three light carriers, and two escort carriers, were damaged badly enough to have to be sent to various facilities for repairs. Almost 150 aircraft were wrecked, blown overboard, or deliberately jettisoned because they were on fire. Vessels in the task force conducted an amazing search-and-rescue operation, even as the storm raged, locating many of the survivors of the lost destroyers.

Even so, almost eight hundred men died.

It would not be a merry Christmas for Admiral Bull Halsey. A week after the storm, the navy convened a court of inquiry in Ulithi, aboard the destroyer tender USS *Cascade* (AD-16). The investigation was of such significance that Admiral Nimitz was in attendance. After hearing testimony, the court ruled that Halsey had certainly committed an "error of judgement" that was likely due to "the stress of war operations" when he sent the Third Fleet into the heart of a strengthening typhoon. However, the panel stopped short of recommending any sort of sanction. Halsey would continue to serve as the Third Fleet commander.

Some good came from the disaster. At the urging of Nimitz, the navy improved its meteorological unit and eventually formed the Joint Typhoon Warning Center. Additionally, as other territories in the Pacific region came under Allied control—such as Manila, Okinawa, and Iwo Jima—weather stations were among the first facilities to be established at each location. And new central weather coordinating offices were opened on Guam and Leyte.

The curse of the typhoon was not quite finished with Bull Halsey, though. Later, while his fleet was supporting the invasion of Okinawa in June 1945, he once again tried to steer his ships out of the path of a building storm but actually sent them directly into its fury. This time, though, only six men died. Seventy aircraft were lost, but no ships. Another court of inquiry suggested Halsey be reassigned, but Nimitz would have none of it. Halsey remained in his command through the end of the war in August 1945.

Even so, the tragic events would result in the storms forever being known as "Halsey's Typhoons."

Dixie Kiefer had a ringside seat for all this drama, as his ship arrived back in Ulithi on Christmas Eve 1944. They had to get in line for repair of the minor damage the carrier had suffered. But Captain Dixie had to have felt relieved, knowing that soon he and his ship could once again concentrate on pummeling the enemy, hastening the end of the war, preparing for the eventual invasion of the Home Islands that everyone now anticipated. Scuttlebutt was that such a massive and deadly assault might possibly take place before the end of the coming year.

Again, Kiefer had to be pleased with his crew and how well they had survived the "divine wind"—both the vicious suicide attacks so far and the ravages of the deadly and destructive typhoon.

All was right with the world. The Big T and her resilient skipper remained amazingly durable.

Chapter Twelve

Out of the Sun

Task Force 38 and all of its aircraft carriers—including *Ticonderoga*—were tied up in Ulithi, Caroline Islands, for just over a week. That was how long it would take to fix the damage Typhoon Cobra had perpetrated on many of the vessels. This narrow volcanic atoll had been a Japanese weather station and outpost until late 1943, when they abandoned the area. As the naval war was pushed westward by the Allies, Admiral Nimitz began looking for a base of operations closer to the Philippines, Formosa, New Guinea, China, and, of course, the Japanese Home Islands.

The harbor at Ulithi Atoll fit the bill, but only after a tremendous effort by the unsung heroes, the Seabees, to construct facilities so the navy could take advantage of the natural harbor there. This project was one of the most closely guarded secrets of the war, and it gave the US Navy a tremendous advantage in the region. There were only relatively minor attacks by Japanese aircraft for the duration of the war, although one of them, in March 1945, struck the carrier USS *Randolph* (CV-15). She was one of *Ticonderoga*'s sister *Essex*-class flat tops. The big ship was at anchor at Ulithi when she was hit by a kamikaze one evening as her crew watched a movie on her flight deck, leaving 27 dead and 105 injured.

Much of the activity at Ulithi was in support of the task forces involved in the invasion of the Philippines, the attacks on Formosa, and the preparations for taking Okinawa. One Seabee later observed, "It was the largest anchorage known to man in the history of planet Earth."

At one point, more than six thousand shipfitters, welders, carpenters, and electricians were stationed in Ulithi, manning repair ships, destroyer tenders, and floating dry docks. One ship had an air-conditioned optical shop and a metal fabrication shop that allowed her crew to manufacture any alloy, making them capable of crafting practically any part that was needed. Another ship, which most resembled a big oiler/tanker, made freshwater from non-potable water and had a full bakery aboard, offering delicious bread and pies. There was even an ice-cream barge that cranked out thousands of gallons of dessert each day. Maybe the most popular spot, though, was the nearby small island of Mogmog, with its sugar-white beach, green-hued surf, and towering palm trees, a perfect site for war-weary sailors to enjoy the tropical weather and waters.

From a tactical standpoint, the base in the Carolines was stellar. From there, fleet oilers could travel out to rendezvous with warships at sea, servicing them while they remained only a relatively short distance from their combat operational areas. Before the war, the Japanese had assumed that the vastness of the Pacific Ocean and the distance American ships would have to travel from Pearl Harbor and the West Coast would make it very difficult for the US Navy to compete way out there. However, with the Ulithi base available to refit, repair, and resupply—including quickly fixing those vessels damaged in the typhoon—many of the Allied ships could deploy for more than a year without having to return to Pearl Harbor or the West Coast of the United States. That was something the Imperial Japanese Navy would never have considered possible when they struck what they believed to be a death knell in Hawaii on December 7, 1941.

Just as Midway had become critical as a perfectly located base for American submarines, Ulithi had become crucial for almost every other kind of warship in the US Navy.

It is understandable, though, that the men aboard Big T soon grew bored. They were accustomed to almost constantly launching and recovering aircraft, manning guns, working on planes, keeping the ship running, and caring for the crew's daily needs. The consensus was that the brisk action the new carrier had been a part of so far was wreaking havoc on the enemy. But now, with their participation in the war paused

Five aircraft carriers at anchor at Ulithi, Caroline Islands. *Ticonderoga* is in the far distance, fifth from the foreground.

because of the storm, they were afraid they might lose their edge. They seemed to have the Japanese befuddled. But just when they might be able to press on, they were participating in endless card games, taking swim call, and overdosing on ice cream.

In truth, there was very little to do on the skinny little atoll besides look at palm trees, swim in the surf, play acey-deucey, and participate in Captain Dixie's constant drills. There weren't even any natives with whom they could consort. When the navy took over Ulithi Atoll, everyone living there was relocated to other islands for their own safety (and to maintain as much secrecy about the new operations base as possible).

Once more, it was Dixie Kiefer's job to keep morale from flagging. Those with jobs to do were to keep doing them, including assisting in repairs. Many kept busy using stencils and paintbrushes to put up on the flat walls of the island structure the colorful insignias for each type of claimed ship and plane they had destroyed. Others had the less glamorous job of scraping paint, slathering on a new gray coat, inspecting lines, and testing systems, along with the thousand other jobs on a ship the size of *Tico*.

African American crewmembers on *Ticonderoga* relax while off watch.

Those who were idled or off-duty, like the flight crewmen, were encouraged to rest, relax, and be ready when they were once again searching out, diving on, and shooting at the enemy. And, of course, being shot at. It would only be a week or so, and they were far from home on Christmas, but they had to remain ready.

Dixie used the ship's PA several times to fuss about slow response in drills or general complacency. He also had to remind the crew of his promise that they would make it to Honshu, the island where Tokyo lay, and that they would soon drop their "hook in Yokohama," in Tokyo Bay.

The ships in the task force were sufficiently repaired so they could steam away only two days before the arrival of 1945. It was quite a sight as seven fleet carriers and six light carriers, along with the fleet's battleships, cruisers, and destroyers, all pulled out, bound for a point in the Philippine Sea. From there, they would be tasked once again with providing air cover in support of the invasion of Luzon in the Philippines. But now they would also be pounding enemy emplacements and airfields on the island of Formosa. In addition, they could continue to restrict shipping headed from Malaysia, the Dutch East Indies, and the Philippines to Japan, filled with raw materials to prolong the war. They were also to send to the bottom those vessels that were loaded with supplies and munitions from the Home Islands on the way to support troops desperately trying to hold on to the Philippines.

The weather had once again turned ugly. There were frequent storms, low clouds, heavy rain, blustery winds. Nothing of the magnitude of Cobra, but still a hindrance to the efforts of everyone in the task force. If there was an upside, it was that the nasty conditions kept the enemy grounded as well. Even so, *Ticonderoga*'s officers, sailors, and flying crews were quickly growing frustrated again.

It was January 6 before the first serious attacks could be launched from the decks of the big carrier. Planes roared off and successfully struck airfields on Luzon. In all, they took out thirty-two enemy aircraft that day. There were more fruitful assaults the next day. Then the ship steamed hard that night to get into position to send attackers to the Ryukyus, a strand of volcanic and coral islands that included Okinawa, stretching from Taiwan to Japan. This was in early preparation for the upcoming Battle of Okinawa that would begin in April, a campaign so intense that both sides dubbed it "The Typhoon of Steel."

But when the time came for *Ticonderoga* to launch, it was a no-go. The weather had turned sour yet again. No pilot could shoot or bomb what he could not see. The attacks on the Ryukyus were canceled and, instead, the Big T's planes headed west, toward Formosa.

Over the next few days, Kiefer's aircrews, along with the others from the carriers in TF-38, operated from west of the Luzon Strait, searching out enemy shipping and sinking anything they could find. Employing more than eight hundred aircraft, the task force sank forty-four ships on January 12 alone.

But then it was three more days of putting up with heavy seas and gale-force winds simply to do the most basic things. Everything from cooking to refueling the ships in the midst of pounding waves, with men on deck tied with ropes to something solid to keep from getting washed overboard. And, of course, not being able to spot a single worthy target, on the seas or in the air, or drawing close enough to bomb anything on the ground. The next few days after that were hit or miss as well. They managed a few raids on Japanese airfields on the Chinese coast, but there was far too much time spent with aircrews languishing in their ready rooms and bunks, waiting for the latest storm clouds to blow over. Once again, seas were too rough for replenishment of any kind. Fuel and food would have to wait for a break in the incessantly bad weather.

The lone positive amid all the frustrations and danger of bad weather was that the same challenges hampered the enemy as well. Not even the dreaded kamikazes could do their evil work in such torturous elements.

Finally, the morning of Sunday, January 21, dawned with bright, brilliant sunshine. The seas were still rough, but planes could fly, even if the headwinds were brutal. And they did fly. During the previous night, the ships in *Ticonderoga*'s task group had steamed back through the Luzon Strait and now floated, mostly within sight of each other, between the Philippines and Formosa. The command came early for pilots to man their planes. Raids were launched at first daylight from the various carriers, sent off to strike targets on Formosa and in the Pescadores, the small islands between Formosa and the Chinese coast. Much of the assault that morning was concentrated on ships in a key harbor on the island. As they completed their run, they could see many vessels ablaze, and the flight crews happily turned back toward the safety of their floating airport, several hundred miles out at sea.

Everyone, including Dixie Kiefer, knew the importance of controlling Formosa. From there, the Allies would have a prime location to strangle the shipping lanes between Japan and the Empire's other outposts and supply sources. And from which to prepare for the eventual invasion of

Captain Dixie on the bridge of *Ticonderoga*.

the Home Islands. The flight crews off the carriers were certainly doing their part to make that control a reality.

Everyone's mood was as sunny as the weather as each plane returned to the carrier with reports of success, of inflicting damage on enemy ships. Later in the morning, as each plane safely set back down on the carrier decks and stopped abruptly when their tail hooks snagged the cable, there were excited reports of victory, of hellish damage unleashed. But first each plane was shoved out of the way for the next aircraft to settle down, and they were pushed either to a parking spot on the flight deck or to the giant elevators to be taken down to the hangar deck. Regardless of the location of the parking spot, crewmen sprang to action, reloading, inspecting, refueling, repairing, preparing the birds for the next attack wave, later in the day, even as other planes were being launched, taking all advantage while the weather was so fine for such activity.

Some crewmen had the job of keeping up with which—and how many—planes left on each run. Then, as everyone landed, they could check off the returnees on their list to see whether they had all come back. And if they had not, who they were. So far, the news was good, and spirits were high as everyone prepared for the next wave to be ready to soar off the deck, catching the cool, continuous wind beneath their wings.

From *Ticonderoga's* Action Report, declassified:

Steaming as before.
    1130. Slowed to 16 knots, changed course to 330 (T).
    1135. Commenced catapulting aircraft "Baker" method, and completed at 1141.
    1142. Commenced deck-launching aircraft and completed at 1145. Commenced steering various courses at various speeds to take station on USS LANGLEY, previously designated as formation guide.

Even though things were going well, Dixie Kiefer could not avoid being worried. He had long since taken to commanding the ship from the open-air bridge, even when his flat top was under general quarters. By regulation, the captain's battle station was supposed to be in a heavily armored pilothouse—the "forward con"—and the executive officer was supposed to be in a similarly protected position in the "after con." Those positions were assigned to help ensure that one or both top officers survived an attack and would be able to oversee recovery.

Captain Dixie, however, felt strongly that he needed to be at a position during tough times where he could be more easily reached by men reporting on damage and other urgent situations. It would be better for him to command from a location where he could directly observe what was happening, what his men were doing, and how the ship was operating. From which he could even communicate with men on the deck below by shouting, if need be. A cramped, isolated cave, shut off from the action, was no place for a hands-on skipper to be when he took his ship into battle.

Hell, he might as well have been back in Pearl Harbor, giving orders by radio from a cabana on the beach!

There was one other thing, and he saw it as the most important consideration about where he was physically located during GQ. He wanted his men to be able to see their captain, see how he was reacting to what was happening, to know that he was not dodging and hiding while his crew risked life and limb fighting fire and shooting ack-ack at incoming attackers.

Dixie Kiefer refused to be locked up and out of sight. He preferred to be visible to his men as he took control and calmly responded to the challenges they all faced together as one tightly melded fighting unit.

So that was why Captain Dixie was where he was on the morning of January 21, 1945. He stood there in the open-air bridge, wearing a helmet and flak vest, binoculars to his eyes as he watched returning planes roll to a sudden stop on the deck below, as men efficiently and enthusiastically went about their jobs, as lookouts scanned the sky for possible enemy ships or planes or the periscope of a submarine.

It was this especially nice weather that had put the worried look on Dixie Kiefer's round face. This good weather that now allowed his aircraft to successfully fly also meant the enemy could get their own torpedo and dive-bombers into the air. And more of those damned suicide planes, too.

Kiefer was aware of at least one new base over on Formosa from which the kamikazes might be able to take off. *Ticonderoga's* planes had been trying to hit it for days, but the rain and wind and fog had kept them from doing it.

That base was at Tainan, on the west coast of the island, on the South China Sea. The kamikaze group established there had been dubbed the "Niitaka Unit" by the Japanese, named for a Formosan mountain peak. The unit had only been christened three days before, the ceremony held in a driving rainstorm. Now, with the weather perfect and a solid report in hand confirming the presence of a big enemy task force—including large carriers—to the southeast, the pilots would finally have the opportunity to sacrifice themselves for the glory of their Empire and its sacred emperor.

Admittedly, the pilots were inadequately trained. Pilots of all kinds were getting difficult to replace considering the escalating losses. So were aircraft. The unit's flight operations officer, Commander Tadashi Naka-jima, was worried about how they would perform. He feared they might make novice mistakes that would get them spotted and intercepted and shot down long before they reached their targets. Only the escorts were trained in aerial combat. The kamikaze knew little more than how to take off and how to aim for and crash into targets.

He watched as three sections of the attack unit—made up of Suisei bombers and Zero fighters, ten attackers and six escorts, a total of sixteen planes—rolled away in planned order. There were reports of American planes in the area. His pilots would have to form up near the wave tops and race away quickly to avoid being seen and attacked before they even got out of sight of the base. The young Japanese suicide pilots would have no chance if they were sighted short of the targeted carriers.

Sure enough, Nakajima's second section, six aircraft, was late leaving for some reason and encountered enemy Grumman Hellcats west of the spine of mountains that bisected the island. Inexperienced or not, that unit managed to keep the Americans occupied just long enough so the other two groups could fly away toward the open sea to the south/southeast.

Meanwhile, back at Task Force 38, Dixie Kiefer had just taken the opportunity to once again remind his men to be especially vigilant. Radar was still not operating completely up to snuff due to the damage to its antenna during Typhoon Cobra. Air cover pilots were once again urged to be extra alert for possible kamikazes. So were the other planes headed to and returning from their targets. The best defense against the suicide planes was to see them early and shoot them down or divert them before they got close to the task force, making them use up their limited supply of fuel to dodge and duck. Then, if they still made it through the air cover, put up a hailstorm of antiaircraft fire from the ships' guns to try to fulfill the crazy pilots' death wishes before they had the opportunity to take an aircraft carrier or other vessel with them to their rendezvous with their revered ancestors.

Kiefer was now convinced there would be an attack on the task force this day. He could feel it in his rather sizable gut. The Japanese were likely as frustrated by the foul weather as his own team had been. They would certainly want to take advantage of the good flying conditions to try to send the Allies scrambling. To once again take out a US aircraft carrier.

Ticonderoga executive officer William Burch and Captain Dixie Kiefer.

Even so, the captain resisted the impulse to go to general quarters prematurely. That gnawing in his gut was not a good enough reason. Gun crews were already in position, in a state of readiness. Lookouts were watching the bright sky. The radar operators were doing the best they could with what they had. And the truth was that everyone on the ship could far more efficiently recover and prepare to launch the next bunch of aircraft—the primary task at hand—if everything was operating in a mostly normal state of readiness, not with men off at far-flung parts of the ship, on edge, anticipating an imminent attack that might or might not come. He already had a deck full of planes, getting loaded with ordnance, fully fueled, ready to launch and get back to the work of attacking the airfields and harbors over on Formosa. General quarters right now might unnecessarily delay—somewhat—getting them off the Big T's deck and on their way again.

Besides, many of the crew were in the process of grabbing their midday meal. Sunday religious services were just now finishing up. The men had been working hard. If something happened, better to have them rested, fed, and spiritually refreshed than prematurely scattered about the ship, nervously anticipating but, in reality, doing nothing if no attack came.

The rain-washed air was fresh and clean, surprisingly cool for that part of the world, even in January. The sun was bright, climbing toward straight overhead as noontime approached. Sailors were lining up on the mess deck for the midday meal. Sundays were special, usually with fried chicken and all the helpings of pie anyone wanted. Those men who were off duty were playing cards, writing letters, catching a nap. Some were even shirtless, sunning themselves on the far reaches of the flight deck. A few were still busy, landing a few straggling aircraft returning from the morning's raids or the occasional covering plane coming down for fuel and new crewmembers.

Dixie Kiefer nervously glanced up at the sun, enjoying the warmth on his face even if the breeze had a touch of cold bite to it. It felt wonderful after all the chilly rain and sea-churning wind of the last few weeks.

But a harsh truth troubled him.

It was a fact that on such a nice day, they could see an approaching aircraft from miles and miles away. But if an attack came, especially a kamikaze, the suicide pilot would be savvy enough to come at them directly out of that bright, warming orb. With few clouds in which to hide, a hell-bent-on-dying pilot would use the sun to assist him in surprising his target.

As Kiefer watched his deck crew and pilots land the last couple of planes and hustle them below to the hangar deck for refueling, as they sent other birds skyward, the captain had another thought. The Japanese—regular attack planes and kamikaze alike—often followed American planes back to the carriers that had launched them in the first place. That made targets easy to locate, even if they did not already know the big task force was out there.

Kiefer wiped the sweat from his face with his handkerchief. It was getting warmer and the flak vest was binding. He once again contemplated going to general quarters–antiaircraft, or even to full-blown attack status, just in case. His gut was arguing with him again.

Dixie was just about to tell his XO, Bill Burch, that he was going to ruin everyone's lunch and bring an abrupt end to the sunbathing.

Just then, the communicator at his elbow crackled to life.

The young sailor's voice on the tinny speaker was just short of frantic.

CHAPTER THIRTEEN

General Quarters

"BOGIE! BOGIE! TEN DEGREES OFF THE STARBOARD BOW!"

Steaming as before.
1205. Went to torpedo defense when bogie was reported.

From his perch in the open bridge, Dixie Kiefer could already hear the screaming of the enemy dive-bomber's engine over the report that came in on the communicator. But he could not see a damn thing. The bastard was coming at them from out of the sun. The blindingly brilliant sun.

"General quarters! Battle stations!" he shouted, and the *bong bong bong* reverberated up and down the full length of the massive vessel. The response was immediate.

Down in the chow hall, some of the men grabbed their sandwiches or chicken legs as they bolted away—it might just be another drill, so why waste good food—but everyone scrambled without hesitation, headed for their assigned battle-station positions. Such a spot ranged from manning guns to standing by a critical valve deep in the ship's innards.

But then, almost immediately, and to confirm the seriousness of the alert, they could hear their own antiaircraft guns commence firing. Many could tell from the sound which ones were blasting away already. And it meant this was no drill. They were under attack.

All over the ship men rushed to where they were supposed to be whenever those *bong*s and the accompanying bugle rang out. Some had a long way to run. Some ladders were traffic jams—up or down—so they sought other routes to get from one deck to another.

Others, like the pilots and other flying crewmembers, had no GQ assignment. They could remain either in their quarters or in the ready room. If needed, and if they suffered a hit, they could eventually go find something to do to help. But for now, they were supposed to stay out of the way.

For his part, Dixie Kiefer knew before he even spotted their attacker that it was a kamikaze. The enemy aircraft was alone, not in formation with anyone else. He was coming fast. And he was lining up on the ship's bow, not broadside like a torpedo bomber would most likely do to enhance his ability to hit the targeted vessel with his deadly fish. Kiefer could already hear the attacker shooting, strafing, doing all the damage he could before ultimately crashing into his target.

"Suicide plane!" one of the lookouts reported, confirming Dixie's suspicions. "Straight off the bow, coming this way!"

Approaching Japanese kamikaze aircraft takes fire. Note shells hitting the water to attempt to disrupt the plane's flight.

"Give him all you got, boys. Make him have to fly through a wall of bullets to get at us," Dixie said, but it was under his breath. No one could have heard him anyway, what with all the noise from his ship's gun crews and those aboard their adjacent escort vessels. Now, too, he could see more enemy planes in the distance, like orderly but very angry bees, possibly forming up for more traditional air attacks or to engage covering fighters and keep them from harassing the kamikazes.

Then the nearest lone plane was close enough that Kiefer no longer needed the binoculars to see him. The Japanese pilot had lined up perfectly, straight ahead, clearly intent on hitting the carrier's flight deck, likely somewhere just aft of the bow. That would do at least enough damage to make it impossible for planes to land and take off from *Tico*. And if the kamikaze could strike at a sharp enough angle, he could go all the way through to the hangar deck below, his bombs potentially doing massive damage, possibly starting fires and setting off explosions among the bombs and torpedoes and fuel stored down there or already loaded on waiting aircraft. That would do the most damage. Maybe even enough to sink the massive ship, but certainly enough to put her out of the war for a bit.

And for that purpose and possibility, the son of a bitch was more than willing to gloriously die.

Still, Kiefer could not imagine how anyone might be able to penetrate all those bullets and shrapnel between the rapidly approaching attacker and the carrier. The narrowing gap was thick with hot metal. It was a brutal curtain of deadly ordnance, surely enough to deflect the enemy pilot no matter how determined he was to die.

Now some of *Ticonderoga*'s gunners were employing a recently learned trick—deliberately aiming at the surface of the sea, kicking up geysers that would be more than strong enough to disrupt the plane's flight if he came in low, as the suicide pilots often tended to do. And if he flew higher to avoid the water, he would be a better target for the other guns, from both carrier and escorts.

The gun crews were applying other hard-learned lessons, too. Firing in bursts to save ammo and keep from overheating gun barrels. Being patient, ensuring the enemy planes were within range before shooting.

Captain Dixie allowed himself just a moment of pride in his fine bunch of boys who were so bravely defending their ship.

> 1209. USS LANGLEY reported a bomb hit. Opened fire on enemy plane on starboard quarter with all guns that would bear.
> 1210. Went to general quarters. Enemy plane dived through the flight deck and gallery spaces forward of the bridge. The plane is thought to have carried a large bomb or explosive charge.

Then, out of the corner of his eye, Kiefer saw a quick flash of flames in the far distance, across an expanse of sea. *Langley* was out there, maybe three-quarters of a mile away. (This was not the original CV-1, the converted coal-hauler and the navy's first aircraft carrier, but the CVL-27, a light carrier in service for almost two years.) She might have been hit by a kamikaze. Or by a bomb or torpedo. But there was no time to watch her, to figure out how she was faring, to see how effectively the rest of the ships in the task force were fighting back.

Ticonderoga had her own problem, and it was coming directly at her, out of the sun at better than three hundred miles per hour. Now the skipper could see the tracers from the plane's guns, even in the dazzling sunshine. And tracers from his own ship's guns, many of them seemingly hitting the approaching Zero head-on. But, amazingly, they were having no effect on the suicide flier.

How in hell did the bastard keep flying—keep coming? How in hell?

It struck Kiefer again just how frustrating it was trying to stop a warrior who fully intended to die, who had no incentive to try to save himself or his airplane to fight another day. Whose sole mission was to crash hard and unleash mayhem.

Below, on the mess deck, John Cox was just finishing the midday meal after his time on the 4:00 a.m. watch. He heard the GQ alert and the almost simultaneous firing of his ship's antiaircraft guns. He dropped his tray and ran for the ladder that led up to the hangar deck. From there, he would need to sprint aft to the ship's fantail, where he was supposed to man one of Big T's quad forty-millimeter guns as his battle station. Just as he ran out onto the hangar deck, he heard and felt the concussion from a massive explosion, somewhere behind him, toward the bow. Metal shrapnel ominously whistled and rattled past him, followed immediately by tongues of flame. A wall of impenetrable smoke chased and overtook him.

Amazingly, none of the flying metal hit Cox, though it did chop down another man or two running alongside him. Cox hurried on in a crouch, as much to get away from the blast as to make it to his battle station. He stepped around or jumped over several of his shipmates who were lying there on the deck—injured, maybe dead. There was already lots of blood.

Cox made it to his gun station. But he and his crew could not see from their perspective anybody close enough to shoot at. The sky from their point of view was empty. But smoke billowed throughout the hangar deck all the way out to the stern of the ship, at the fantail. There was obviously plenty of fire up there somewhere toward the bow of the carrier. Cox could only hope there were enough of his shipmates left alive so they could snuff it out before it reached the mass of the loaded planes. Or even worse, the magazine down low in the bowels of the ship.

He waited for something to shoot at. And he prayed.

Many of *Ticonderoga*'s aircraft-preparation crewmen were working on planes on both the hangar and flight decks, getting them set for that afternoon's missions. Those on the flight deck, attending to planes arrayed from near the island aft, were stunned to see the Japanese kamikaze zooming straight for them.

But then, at the last instant, the pilot lifted the nose slightly, turned a bit, and steered instead toward the forward elevator. Several sailors would later report that the big up-and-down platform had just started down with a plane loaded aboard. They could only speculate that the enemy flier saw that as an opportunity to get to the lower deck and do more damage down there, where gas hoses and ordnance would be more plentiful.

Though many of the men working at the planes topside were hurt or killed by the crash and subsequent bomb detonation, that last-second swerve by the Zero likely saved many lives. There is no way to know how much explosion and fire would have been unleashed had he crashed into the three dozen fully loaded and fueled planes grouped together there on the flight deck.

Lieutenant Harold Butcher, one of the Hellcat pilots, had just pulled on his flight suit and was preparing to leave the ready room, heading up to the flight deck to climb into his plane and head back toward Formosa. That was when he heard the racket of the twenty-millimeter guns start up just as the GQ Klaxon sounded. He stopped, waited, not wanting to be in the way of men who would already be racing for their battle stations.

Then there was a sudden staggering blast so loud and close it threatened to knock him off his feet. Almost instantly there was thick, black smoke pouring from the ventilation ducts inside the ready room. The pilots all looked at each other.

They had been hit. Bomb, torpedo, kamikaze—it did not really matter.

Without even thinking, Butcher stepped outside onto the catwalk to take a look. On the far end of the hangar deck, several planes were already afire, just visible through the smoke. There were bodies on the deck. Parts of bodies, as well.

Butcher could make out through the smoke that men were already manning fire hoses, spraying foam, even though there were more

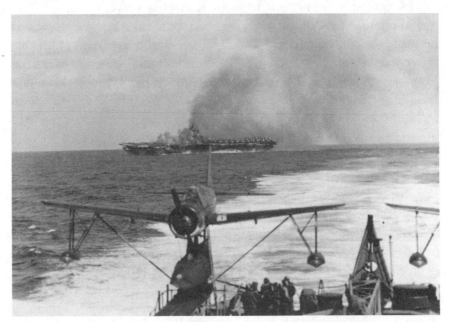

Ticonderoga on fire, as seen from the light cruiser USS *Miami* (CL-89).

explosions still occurring, smaller but powerful. A smoking ball of hot metal rolled to a stop on the catwalk just a few feet away from where he stood. He started to go get it, assuming it came from whatever plane or bomb that had struck the ship. It might make a good souvenir. Then he thought better of it.

> 1212. Lost a man overboard on starboard side.
> 1220. Changed course left to 290 (T) to aid fighting the fire in the hangar deck.
> 1222. The Captain ordered a 5 [degree] list to port to aid fire fighting.
> 1225. Bogie reported overhead.
> 1226. Lost man overboard on port side.
> 1230. Maneuvering on various courses to keep free water from hoses to port side.
> 1231. More bogies reported in immediate vicinity. Continued firing at enemy plane diving on ESSEX.
> 1239. Sprinkled forward magazines.
> 1241. Ceased firing.
> 1241. Lost man overboard on starboard quarter.
> 1246. Steadied on course 330 (T).

Deck guns were still pounding away at targets. A destroyer raced past, dangerously close, Butcher thought, but her guns, pointed upward, were blasting away as well. Butcher could hear the screaming of a diving plane—another kamikaze!—but then there was nothing. No more plane. No thundering blast. They must have gotten him—he had disintegrated or was in the drink.

Butcher ducked back into the ready room with some of the other pilots.

"Kamikaze?" somebody asked.

"Had to be," Butcher confirmed. "Hit the flight deck at the forward elevator and looks like his bombs did lots of damage up there. And there are more of 'em out there."

The last observation was obvious. The throbbing of gunfire continued, as insistent as ever, and they were certainly shooting at something that posed further threat.

There was really nothing for the aircrews to do. Their raid was postponed at best, likely scrubbed. There was nothing they were supposed to be doing if they could not get to their planes and take off. Nobody would think less of them—even those supposed to fly fighters and engage the attackers—if they simply remained in a safe place and rode out whatever was happening. Pilots were hard to come by, not easily replaced.

"Being without anything to do to help during an attack is hell," Butcher later said. He could not tolerate sitting idly by in the smoky ready room. He eventually went out and pitched in, passing canisters of foam to replenish the foamite generators, assisting in tossing bombs and torpedoes overboard, and helping with wounded and dead men.

He knew these men would do just about anything for him and the other flying crewmembers. He wanted to do the same for them.

Throughout the ship, speakers crackled with reports of fire, damage, death, and destruction. Then, amid all the voices, there was Captain Dixie on the communicator.

"Men, do your jobs! Don't panic. If you don't have a job, help somebody else do his. Get the bombs and rockets disarmed. Get them off the planes and over the side. If you can get close enough, roll any damaged or burning planes over the side. Don't let fire get to any ordnance. Dump it overboard. Gun crews, shoot anything that has a meatball on it. Do what you have been trained to do. We're in good shape. We will be in good shape!"

Over on the *Langley*, less than a mile off *Ticonderoga*'s port bow, Louis Giroir was in his ship's galley when he heard a big boom toward the bow of the vessel, followed by the immediate call to general quarters. He instantly headed for the light carrier's air group ready room, assuming they would want to put some more fighters in the air if they were under attack. But along the way, he glanced over toward the Big T.

Giroir had a special interest in the larger flat top. He had been among the ship's original crew when she was commissioned, only transferring off her before Christmas 1944, after the typhoon. He had just recently been assigned to duty on *Langley*. He still had many friends over there on that big girl. Such loyalty ran deep. He was at the least just as concerned about his buddies over there as he was with those on his new ship.

Crewmen survey damage to Big T's hangar deck after kamikaze attack.

He watched as the kamikaze pilot flew through a haze of bullets, seemingly undeterred, and plunged at a sharp angle into the *Ticonderoga*'s flight deck, just aft of the bow. He could not hear Captain Kiefer's assessment on the PA of his ship's chances, but based on what Giroir was seeing, even from that far away, he would not have agreed with Captain Dixie that they were all right over there.

"I could see huge columns of flames escaping through openings between the flight deck and the hangar deck," he later related. "Explosions were seen on both decks, apparently from aircraft gasoline tanks. I saw five-inch aerial rockets flying into space along with tracer bullets heading toward no apparent target. The ship was an inferno."

Even so, Giroir noticed that the big carrier's guns continued firing "a halo of impenetrable antiaircraft fire." He watched as they chased off two attackers and shot down another. Though impressed to see "the ship so full of fight" throughout the attack, Giroir turned his attention back to his own vessel to see what he could do to help. Turns out his ship had been struck by two bombs, not a kamikaze, and the damage was relatively minor.

But, whenever Giroir had a chance, he looked across the way to try to see how his old ship and his many friends were doing. He could only say a prayer on their behalf. It appeared to him that they needed plenty of divine help over there.

Back on *Ticonderoga*, Carl Clement was on his way down to the chief petty officers' mess to grab a sandwich before helping to launch more bombers to attack Formosa. He had just stepped through the hatch and was going down the ladder when almost simultaneously the ship's guns began firing and he heard the announcement and clanging for general quarters.

Clement spun around and was on his way to his battle station, on the hangar deck, to make certain the sprinklers were ready in case of fire amid the planes there. That was when a tremendous blast knocked him to the deck. It was a while later before he learned that a kamikaze plane had crashed into Big T's flight deck, its bombs exploding and doing most of the damage directly below where it hit, on the hangar deck at the elevator.

When Clement was able to stand, he made his way as far forward as he could before the flames and smoke stopped him. Some of the sprinklers were working, but others were not. He had no tools to get them going, so he got busy instead helping wounded men to the sick-bay hatch. Then he joined other shipmates as they furiously unattached and dropped to the deck bombs that were already loaded on aircraft, ready for the afternoon's raids. Then they hastily rolled or carried them to the side and tossed them into the sea. They even shoved a few damaged and burning aircraft over the side as well.

Time after time, Clement witnessed men toting bombs they should not have been able to lift. Carrying them through smoke—and sometimes fire—to the edge of the deck and somehow getting them thrown overboard. There was no explanation for such superhuman strength other than "they had to." If any one of those bombs had exploded, the damage and carnage would have been exponentially greater.

Clement was hearing reports all around him that the water from the sprinklers and fire hoses was washing gasoline down hatches to lower decks, spreading the fires below. There were no built-up barriers around the hatches, so anything that was liquid simply drained downward, seek-

Captain Kiefer orders an intentional list to port to aid in putting burning planes and bombs as well as blazing fuel into the sea.

ing the lowest level. There was nothing he could do about that at the moment. There were wounded to try to help. More bombs and torpedoes to jettison. Fires to quell.

Then, when he stopped long enough to notice, Carl Clement made a startling discovery: The deck beneath his feet had begun to take on a decided slant. The gigantic carrier was listing noticeably. No wonder it was becoming less difficult to roll some of the heavier weapons to the side and dump them overboard. Gravity and the list were helping.

Again, nothing he could do about that now. He shook his head and worked on.

Don Noyes was also finishing up lunch when he heard the *whump* of the Japanese plane plunging into his ship. He had always had a fear of finding himself trapped belowdecks in a sinking ship, so he jumped over mess tables and fought through the crowd to the nearest ladder leading up. That, too, was the way to his battle station.

"I got to the top of the ladder to find a marine who had been on watch there cut in two by the bomb," he would remember. "Hurrying to my battle station on the flight deck, I found my division commander . . . [had been] cut in half as he came through the island hatch to the flight deck. Fires had broken out everywhere and our job was to keep our own bombs from exploding."

Noyes remembers losing all thirty-five F6F fliers that had been arrayed on the flight deck, ready to go back to work.

"Those that did not burn we pushed over the side," he recalls.

Aviation ordnanceman William Gowder was busy at work when GQ sounded. He was responsible for the weaponry and gun cameras on eight F6F fighter planes. That job had him right out there on the open flight deck of *Ticonderoga* at midday on January 21, 1945, getting his planes ready to catapult off the carrier once more, headed back for targets on Formosa.

He remembers just how nice the weather was—clear of clouds, visibility virtually unlimited, and a brisk, cool breeze blowing. Gowder was standing on a wing stub of one of his planes as he worked. The wings were still folded up to make more room on the crowded deck. Snapping them down into flying position would be the last thing they would do before the Hellcat pilot revved his engine and the catapult flung him forward.

Just then, a dark shadow passed over Gowder. He looked up. Again, no clouds. No bridges to steam beneath out there in the middle of the ocean. And none of the ships in the task force were yet launching planes.

At that instant, the loud clanging of the GQ alarm and the bugle rang out. Before he could even jump down from his perch, he was rocked by a horrible explosion no more than two hundred feet from where he worked. Gowder held on to keep from being thrown to the deck.

Toward the ship's bow, he could see men flying high into the air, tossed over the side into the sea. His first thought was to rush to the edge of the deck and throw kapok life vests down to them, so he did just that. However, the devices were flat. They had been used so often as cushions for sunbathing and napping that most of them promptly sank.

Then there was fire everywhere. Because of his regular duty, William Gowder was more aware than most that he and his shipmates

Men fight fires on the flight deck after the kamikaze plane strikes near the carrier's elevator.

now stood in the midst of a bunch of highly explosive devices, attached to airplanes, armed, ready to shoot. If they got hot, they could start exploding in a deadly pyrotechnic display. He could already hear .50 caliber shells discharging, but they were relatively benign without a barrel to direct their slugs.

He and others began disarming, dropping free, and carrying small bombs and rolling bigger ones to the deck's edge and tumbling them into the water. They had to load some of the larger bombs onto skids—after they were disarmed—and roll them to the edge, often through burning gasoline.

"That increased the flow of adrenaline substantially," Gowder later recalled.

The burning fuel was a problem everyone noticed. Flaming gasoline spilled down open hatches, allowing fires to spread to the decks below.

The hatches were supposed to have been closed against just such an eventuality while under general quarters, but the attack had come so close upon the call that there had not been time to do so in most cases. Besides, the hatch openings were virtually at deck level, with no lip around them to prevent liquids from pouring in.

At one point, Gowder glanced down and saw a small book on the deck. It was a Japanese-English dictionary, almost certainly the property of the late suicide pilot. Gowder instinctively picked it up and stuck it into a pocket, intending to keep it as a souvenir. Later, all personnel would be asked to turn in such mementos for inspection. Gowder did as ordered and never saw the book again.

The ordnanceman certainly knew just how dangerous all those explosive devices on the ship's flight and hangar decks were. He and his fellow sailors worked tirelessly over the next hour, getting as much of it as they could reach despite the flames and smoke off Big T and then tossing it into the sea, where it would pose no danger. And for once, the crews paid no attention to the type of aircraft or weapons they were working on. Crews usually stuck exclusively to the planes to which they were assigned: fighters, dive-bombers, or torpedo planes. Not that day.

"Everyone helped each other in a marvelous display of teamwork," Gowder later reported. "I believe this is what helped prevent other massive explosions."

There would be many reports of close calls and what-ifs.

"I started up the ladder but a marine shoved me aside and went up ahead of me," one sailor would relate. "When the Jap hit us, [the marine] was at the top of the ladder. He fell back down, decapitated by shrapnel. If he had not pushed me out of the way . . ."

"My buddy and I decided to swap battle stations at the last minute," another man remembers. "He got hit and died. I didn't have a scratch."

"I always was a chow hound. I cut the chow line early that morning so I could eat early and get to my duty quarters," was another sailor's story. "Somebody told me later that if I had eaten when I was supposed to I would have been on the gun that got wiped out and killed everybody."

"I didn't have time to make it to my gun mount, number four, a five-inch open mount on the port side," another Big T sailor recalls. "When I got there, the pointer mechanism had been damaged by something. Had I been there, whatever hit it would [have] gone right through me, too."

At one point, rumors spread that the order had been given by Captain Dixie to abandon ship. Rumors were not commands, the officers reminded those who tended to believe what they were hearing, but especially those who tried to spread such falsehoods. That bit of conjecture was quickly squashed. Though some *Ticonderoga* crewmembers ended up in the water, there is no confirmation that anyone followed any false order to abandon the ship.

Seaman Richard Hodgson had been on the mess deck enjoying his Sunday dinner. He had just grabbed a second piece of pie. He dearly loved the ship's cooks' cherry pie. But before he could take a bite, he heard firing from their own guns and the immediate cacophony of the general quarters alarm. Hodgson dropped his fork but slid the pie into a napkin, intending to eat it on the way to his battle station forward. This was located in what the sailors called "officer country"—the officers' quarters and mess.

Somewhere along the way, he dropped his piece of pie. Also on his way, Hodgson heard a familiar, encouraging voice coming from a speaker nearby. He recognized it as his skipper.

"Keep calm, men," Captain Dixie was saying from his perch up on the open-air bridge. "Don't get excited. Keep calm. Just do your jobs and we'll be okay. Get those shells over the side. Shove the planes into the sea."

Then Hodgson heard and felt a body-numbing explosion. He stumbled, caught hold of something, got his balance, and somehow kept running. There were small fires in the area of the officers' compartments, but the smoke was the big problem. Although the breathing apparatus he found did not seem to function properly, he and his shipmates persevered. They sprayed water on the overhead and bulkheads, already too hot to touch, in an effort to keep fires from spreading down to where they were. They knew they had to keep flames from reaching the magazine. If that happened, the big ship would be a goner.

They kept spraying, kept working, kept fighting, though it was dark and smoky down there. Breathing was near impossible. No matter. They had to get those fires out, or there was a real chance they would be blown to kingdom come—that they would die young and a long, long way from home.

In addition to hearing their captain's voice on the speakers and seeing him leaning out of the bridge to give them a thumbs-up and urge them on, the men were surprised to spot the ship's second-in-command, Bill Burch, the XO, right down there in the heart of the mayhem on the hangar deck. He had come down from the bridge to take a look-see for himself and to report back to Captain Dixie. But first he grabbed a fire hose and waded into the inferno, helping his men fight the blazes.

"Sir?"

"What is it, son?"

"Your shirt's on fire, sir."

Burch calmly stepped into the spray from another fire hose.

"How about now?"

"You're out now, sir."

Then, when they seemed to have gotten the worst of the fire extinguished, Burch had another thought.

"I want to go forward and see what the fire is doing up there. I need some backup," he told a sailor. Several sailors in gas masks volunteered to lead him as far as he wanted to go. Before long, though, Burch had become almost overwhelmed by the dense smoke.

"I think I've seen about all I need to see," he said, coughing and spitting. "Now, can one of you show me how to get back to the bridge? I have to get to the bridge."

The XO had become lost, disoriented in the stifling smoke. One of the sailors offered to show him a back way he knew about that was not obstructed by all the damage. Along the way, the young man noticed that Burch was wet from all the water from the fire hoses and sprinklers. The XO was shivering badly. The sailor grabbed a dungaree jacket he spotted hanging on a hook in the passageway and gave it to the officer.

"Thank you, young man," Burch said with a broad grin. "You may have saved my life there."

Then they reached the bridge, where Burch could give Captain Dixie the rather ominous report. He told the skipper just how dicey the situation was on *Ticonderoga*, how much destruction that lone kamikaze had been able to do to the big vessel.

"Dixie's kids will take care of it," Kiefer responded. "We'll be okay, Bill."

Lieutenant Howard Chamblin, a flier, had been standing next to a plane on the hangar deck alongside reconnaissance pilot Ensign "Shorty" Ewing. They had a map spread out on the aircraft's wing, studying Chamblin's intended targets for the afternoon, each located on the south tip of the island of Formosa. When the guns suddenly kicked off firing and general quarters was declared, the two fliers stepped into the closest enclosed compartment, the nearby photo lab, to wait out whatever was going on.

That was where they were when the suicide plane struck *Ticonderoga* moments later. The walls of the room quickly became too hot to touch. Steam poured from beneath the door. They could smell hot metal and what had to be the stench of burning flesh.

When Chamblin, Ewing, and the four photographers already in the lab tried to open the door and escape, they realized it was jammed. When they tried to force it open, they could see that there were intense flames on the other side, fed by gasoline, and there was no way out of the room. They were trapped right next to a fiery furnace and mere feet from explosive weaponry. In a room equipped with flammable chemicals and photo stock.

In minutes, with the room becoming too hot for them to stay there, Chamblin ordered that the only porthole in the compartment be opened. If there was no other way, they would have to dive into the sea and hope somebody picked them up before the sharks had a feast. First, though, Chamblin leaned out the narrow opening as far as he could. To the left, on the hangar deck, he could see another officer, furiously directing a firefighting party.

The pilot screamed and waved furiously, somehow getting the man's attention. He yelled for him to pass a line over to him. Maybe they could exit from the porthole, swing out over the water and back to the ship's side, and then climb up the rope to the deck. Somehow that seemed far better than jumping all the way down to the water—nearly ninety feet—and then having to hope somebody would see them floating out there and pluck them out of the sea in the middle of a suicide plane attack.

That was how Chamblin and the others escaped the lab. It was during his climb up the slippery one-inch rope that the pilot—the last man out of the sweltering compartment—noticed that *Ticonderoga* had begun to list rather sharply to port. When he was helped up onto the deck, it was all he could do to keep his footing because of the tilt of the ship and the slippery surface.

It has to be a 10-degree list, he thought. *Substantial.*

That could only mean one thing in Chamblin's estimation: *Ticonderoga* was sinking. Fast. And a ship her size going down would take everything aboard—or in the water nearby—with her.

If that was the case, there was not a thing anybody could do about it but ride her down into the depths of an unforgiving sea.

CHAPTER FOURTEEN

The Second Kamikaze

"CAPTAIN DIXIE, SHOULDN'T WE BE ZIGZAGGING?"

Kiefer had watched the kamikaze plow into his flight deck, had seen the explosions, the smoke, the fires. Damage reports were pouring in on the radio, the talk system, from shouted updates by men below him on the deck. But he knew his officers and men were doing all they could to overcome the flames. Now his focus was on getting his ship into the right position so his gun crews might better stave off more suicide planes and a few dive-bombers and fighters that were accompanying them.

"I doubt we could dodge those guys, even as fast as we are. Better we keep steady so the wind will blow the smoke and fire away from the ship, give the damage-control team a chance to get ahead of it." He glanced at some gauges, leaned out the open window, felt the breeze on his face. That information confirmed another thing for Kiefer, and he adjusted accordingly. "Slow to ten knots. We're just fanning the flames with our speed and making it harder for our boys."

Yes, he was doing the unorthodox. But Kiefer knew what it would take to give his crews below a chance. They had to keep the fire away from the magazine and the rest of the aircraft still parked on the two decks.

Then he had another thought.

"Let's flood the port tanks. Take on a list of five degrees as quickly as you can. Let's spill that burning fuel over the side."

"Aye, Captain. But we're getting reports of fuel getting washed down some of the open hatches, spreading the fire down below."

"Damned hatch covers should have been closed when we went to . . . Well, I don't suppose the Japs gave us time, did they?" Kiefer thought for just a moment. "I told 'em in Newport News we should have a lip around the hatches for this very reason. Okay. But we still need to get the burning fuel overboard before it sets every plane on our decks afire. We'll take our chances on the hatches."

He again leaned out the window, yelling encouragement to the gun crews nearby, to the men working on the deck up ahead. No one could hear him, though. It was too noisy. They continued to fire at planes in the air.

> 1250. Commenced firing on enemy plane crossing ahead from port to starboard. Set plane on fire and saw it hit water. Pilot was observed to bail out.
> 1253. Increased speed to 20 knots, 150 rpm.
> 1255. Bogies reported to northward.

Here came another one, barreling in through flak and shells as if there was nothing there at all to stop him. The shooting was coming not just from Big T but also from two nearby destroyers.

Just when it appeared the kamikaze would follow his buddy into the big carrier's deck, a wing on the plane seemed to break away of its own volition, as if it was abandoning the rest of the plane in midair. The Zero's engine erupted into brilliant flames, and it began somersaulting across the sky before plunging into the sea in a fiery, smoking mass.

Kiefer could hear cheers from his men as they paused, waiting for the next plane to come within range. He could not tell whose shells, from the carrier or from one of the destroyers, had actually punched out the Zero, but it did not matter. That one would no longer be a problem.

The skipper checked the ship's clock. It had been forty minutes since the suicide plane had struck his deck and exploded. Gauging from the smoke and the cryptic reports on the communicator, the fire was getting no worse, but not much better. Men were still trapped below. Triage had been set up in sick bay and casualties assessed. Bodies were being stacked on the fantail, out of the way.

The casualty count was going to be high. Tragically high.

Many men had been working up front on the carrier's hangar deck, getting planes ready. When the Japanese plane's bombs exploded, shrapnel had been flung up and down the length of the huge, covered-but-open deck, cutting men down. Then the fires. Men incinerated where they stood. Others burned so badly they likely would not survive.

Still, from all Kiefer could see from his perch and what he was hearing, his crew—officers and sailors alike—were doing remarkably brave things down there. Though there were steam leaks, they still had power. Pumps were all working. The intentional tilting of the ship and the slowed speed—though setting off a mass of rumors among those who were now convinced they were sinking—was finally giving firefighters a hopeful bit of an advantage.

Now, if they could only avoid being hit again. There were reports on the radio of other enemy planes still in the area.

There are varied accounts from the men who were aboard *Ticonderoga* that day regarding exactly what happened, including the amount of time that passed between when the first suicide plane hit them and when the devastating crash of the second one occurred. Some say it was only minutes. Some remember it as hours. The best estimate, and the official time, is almost one hour.

Pharmacist's Mate Robert Childers was helping injured men on the flight deck when someone told him there were a number of sailors who needed assistance in an office on the second level of the ship's island. Fragments had been hurled at them when the first plane exploded. The smoke was so bad in that area that Childers could hardly stay conscious. Even so, he managed to assist several men who had suffered grisly injuries. With enough sulfa powder and pressure bandages to slow the bleeding, they had a chance. Several of the others in the compartment did not make it.

Someone passed down gas masks. As Childers later noted, "They helped a little bit, but our lungs were pretty smoked up by then anyway. We finally yelled for someone to drop us down some lines from the catwalk above and we climbed out of the compartment through a porthole."

They had just stepped into another compartment in the island when they noted a distinctive urgency in all the gunfire from the ship. And the prominent screaming of an aircraft engine getting closer and closer.

Ticonderoga seen seconds after second kamikaze plane struck the carrier's island.

"We watched through the porthole as he was coming in," Childers recalled. "We all hit the deck just before he exploded into the superstructure and gun mounts above us."

Stunned, it took Childers a moment to realize that despite the proximity of the plane's hit, he was not hurt. Nor were the others in the compartment. But there certainly would be more men who had not fared so well. He risked a quick peek out the porthole.

Smoke everywhere. And fire.

The door on the other side of the room had been blown open, and it looked clearer that way. A route to the catwalk. He picked up his medical bag and started out, not sure whether to go up or down. There would be plenty of customers in either direction.

Then, as he stepped outside, he heard a call from someone. Help needed. On the bridge. People badly hurt up there. The captain. The XO. Some of the other senior officers.

Childers headed up as quickly as he could, not even pausing to look back at the structural damage the second suicide bastard had done to

Ticonderoga. He knew he needed to get to work, cleaning up the horrific human damage just as he had been trained to do.

> 1258. Took enemy plane under fire diving in at 5,000 yards at about 2,000 feet altitude. Entire battery bearing and firing with excellent pattern. Failed to stop plane which struck head on at roller path of number one 5" battery director at about 070 [degrees] relative.
>
> Plane evidently carried bombs or explosive charge.
>
> Sky I was demolished and splinters showered down both sides of the island structure and thru adjacent areas, killing and wounding many personnel and setting planes amidships on fire.

Over on the USS *Langley*, Louis Giroir was still watching as the drama intensified on his former ship. He looked on in horror as a kamikaze peeled away from his escort and appeared to be lining up for an attempted strike on Big T. Again, the sky was filled with ack-ack, but the suicide pilot seemed immune to it all. He steered his Zero through the hellish barrier of deadly gunfire, directly at the middle part of the big carrier.

"I saw an explosion and a huge fireball ascend up into the sky," Giroir would recall. "From my vantage point, it appeared that the plane struck the flight deck at the bottom of the island. [An already bad situation] was made worse, more fire and smoke. She was already listing and moving slowly. If there was a third attack, 'The *Ti*' would be sunk for sure."

As Giroir watched, it appeared that this was exactly what was about to happen. A third kamikaze took aim on the stricken vessel, a wounded, vulnerable elephant stalked by jackals. Giroir saw the pilot press home his attack, guns spitting, even as the crews on the carrier kept blasting away at him. The Japanese rolled over, climbed, and then turned back downward, determinedly accelerating his dive.

But then, inexplicably, he pulled up. Maybe he was intimidated by all the antiaircraft attention he was attracting. Maybe he simply wanted to try a different attack angle, to strike a place not already afire and smoking.

At any rate, the enemy plane turned away at the last moment. Then, as soon as he had flown out of range of the ship's guns, two F6F fighters showed up and were on his tail. They quickly shot him out of the sky.

Giroir breathed a big sigh of relief even as he discerned that the situation on the carrier remained ominous. But again, all he could do was hope and pray for his former shipmates out there. And he did plenty of both.

The communications center on the *Ticonderoga* was taken out by the second crash. Radio had to be shifted to the standby Radio #3 in the stern area of the ship. That would take a little while. Everyone both on and off the carrier wanted to know about the captain, the XO, and the rest of the officers. The task force commander quickly learned that the enemy plane had hit the island, or damn close. The kamikaze had bored right into the area where Kiefer and many of the vessel's senior officers had been located. Initial damage and casualty reports had to be relayed visually to the other ships. They were necessarily spotty.

> Numerous fires were started on the island structure.
> The Captain and Executive Officer were wounded and incapacitated. The Navigator took the con.
> Continued maneuvering on various courses at various speeds fighting fires and maintaining approximate position in formation. Increased list to 8 degrees.
> Doubled the bridge lookout.

The medic, Robert Childers, was one of the first to get to the bridge. It was a mess, and he was afraid of what he might find there. Especially when it came to Captain Dixie and his exec, Commander William Burch. He was stunned to find both officers still standing there, still in command, still trying to get reports on how much bloodshed and damage there might have been from the second suicide crash.

Despite their fortitude, it was clear that both men were seriously hurt. So were other officers, including Lieutenant Commander "Ace" Barton, the assistant air officer. Air Officer Commander Claire Miller had been killed, along with Gunnery Officer Commander Herbert Fulmer and Assistant Gunnery Officer Lieutenant Reynolds Bess.

Childers got to Burch first, in the rear open bridge area. Though he was conscious and trying to stay with it, it was obvious the exec needed a stretcher and to go to sick bay right away. Childers called for help, but

Burch insisted on remaining at his post, directing the firefighters down on the deck.

Childers hurried over to the skipper next. It appeared to make Captain Dixie angry when the medic simply asked him how he was doing. The skipper was bleeding badly. Though the flak vest had likely saved his life, shrapnel from the crash just outside his window had left gaping wounds all over his body. His normally ruddy skin was pasty and pale. His right forearm was bent at an odd angle, clearly badly broken, and blood gushed from an open wound near the bone break, as well as another gouge on his forehead.

"Son, can you just put a Band-Aid on it? I need to be paying attention to my knittin' up here 'til we can—"

"Jesus, Captain. Looks like you broke both bones in your right forearm. I'm going to wrap it, but you need to go down to sick bay right now and let them splint—"

"Where's the XO?" Kiefer asked.

"He's . . . uh . . . he's hurt pretty bad. We are taking him down to sick bay."

Sure enough, a stretcher crew had gotten the XO to lie down—against his will—and were about to carry him below.

"While Bill's gettin' seen to, I'll stay on the bridge until we have the fires under control. Until I know we can maintain power and keep moving."

"Then at least stay still so I—sorry, sir—I'll try to stop some of this bleeding. How you feeling, sir? You've lost a lot of blood . . ."

Childers and another man helped Kiefer lie down on a mattress that had appeared from somewhere. The medic worked on his skipper's ghastly broken arm and tried to bandage the gaping gash on his head.

"How are the men below?"

"Uh, lots of casualties, sir. But we got a bunch of them that are just as stubborn as their skipper . . . Sorry again, sir . . . they're staying at their posts, manning hoses, shoving planes and ammo overboard, toting other wounded. They're flat refusing to go to sick bay and get treated. I don't think the navy's going to have enough medals and ribbons for all of them, sir."

"Does not surprise me. Not one damn bit. Every man on this ship is one tough son of a gun. 'Dixie's kids,' I call 'em. Be it typhoon or kamikaze, I've watched what they can do. Ouch!"

"Sorry, sir—it's a compound fracture. Needs to be properly set and splinted . . ."

"After a while. Hey, somebody get me updates from the hangar deck and see what damage control says about the fires down there. They've done a fantastic job. Let's don't lose it now."

"Aye, sir."

"Be sure they know the bridge is well aware of the job they're doing. We're going to save Big T. She's got a lot more to do in this war, and their captain is not going over the side of another carrier if he can help it. I did that stunt already. A fellow could get himself hurt doing that."

"We'll tell 'em, sir."

"Fantastic job, men. Now somebody help me get back up. Let's see how the wind is blowing now."

"Captain, steady. You've lost a lot of . . ."

The skipper seemed woozy but managed to stand there, cradling the wrapped arm to his chest, studying the display in front of him. He looked out, past the smoke billowing from just below them.

"Our position looks good, but there's still lots of fire and smoke on the flight deck and below. Anybody got me an update on the hangar deck, just in case we need to try to get some planes in the air? What's the degree of list by now? Casualty update? Any more guns out of commission? Ammo carriers still keeping them supplied, just in case? Anybody heard how *Langley* is doing? I saw her take some kind of strike, maybe another kamikaze, just before our first hit. Bring speed to twelve knots if we got the power available so the current doesn't keep us floating in that burning oil. Then—"

"Captain, you're going to have to keep pressure on that wound on your face. It's deep and bleeding like a son of a—"

"Will do, but son, I need you to get back down and take care of the boys doing all the work. Tell 'em we got their backs. Show the Japs the Big T is still in this war. She's indestructible. Long as we have a crew that performs like this. Indestructible!"

Childers could not disobey a direct order. He saluted and left the bridge, heading down to try to help more of his shipmates.

Though he never would have let his men know it, Captain Kiefer was now, for the first time, wondering whether they actually would be able to save *Ticonderoga*. There was too much fire. Another attack, a spark that reached the magazine, another set of explosions on the hangar deck, might be all it took to take them down. He had seen such a thing first-hand when it only took a submarine's torpedo to finish off and sink the *Yorktown* from beneath him.

Still, he decided, so long as they were afloat they had a chance. For the men, knowing that their captain persevered—though seriously wounded—and that he was up there on the bridge fighting right along with them became even more important than before.

Kiefer would later learn that Bill Burch had, indeed, been carried on a stretcher to sick bay for attention to his wounds. But along the way, he had asked his bearers to take him by several portions of the ship so he could see for himself how things were going and offer advice and direction to the brave men below. He also wanted to assure everyone that the *Ticonderoga* was still in good hands. That Captain Dixie was still on the bridge, running the ship. That their skipper had, by God, survived an almost direct hit by the enemy plane.

Sometime after the attack, when radio communications were finally cobbled back together, a message was radioed over to the Big T's skipper from the task force commander.

"Are you going to abandon ship?"

Those who were on the bridge that day report that Kiefer became enraged when he read the message. He instructed his radio operator to respond with a two-word reply: "Hell no."

> 1415. All fires under control. Commenced taking list off ship.
> 1439. The largest fire which was on the second deck was extinguished.
> 1510. Fire broke out in CIC spaces and was extinguished at 1520.

And just as he said he would, Dixie Kiefer remained on the bridge, overseeing damage control and guiding the ship, even as he officially put

Mangled island structure after second kamikaze hit on *Ticonderoga*.

Big T's third-senior officer in charge. The skipper had more than sixty wounds all over his body from the debris that had flown throughout the compartment—first, when the second plane had crashed into the island, and then again an instant later, when its bombs exploded. Many of those lacerations would require stitches, shrapnel would have to be dug out, and he would lose even more blood. His right arm was badly broken, the pain surely intense.

Even so, he refused all efforts to make him leave the bridge and seek medical attention until he was certain the fires were out on his ship. He also kept shooing the medics away when they would try to help him, insisting they concentrate on his "kids" down there who needed attention far more than he did.

At around 2:00 p.m., even though most of the threatening flames had been extinguished, Kiefer insisted on remaining in command as darkness fell. This way, he could make sure Big T was properly rigged for night running. He wanted to minimize the chance a submarine or another dive-bomber might happen upon his slow vessel and finish the job.

All lights were to be extinguished, partly because they were now operating under greatly reduced power. And due to damage to the boilers and plumbing, they could steam at a speed of only a little less than ten knots until they could get boilers repaired and back online. Suicide planes were no longer a threat in the darkness, but submarines or bombers certainly were, if they could see the ship, because the big flat top was now a virtual sitting duck.

Besides, there were still plenty of salvage, repair, and search-and-rescue efforts going on aboard *Ticonderoga*. There had been thousands of men on his ship who had worked tirelessly through the attacks and their aftermath. Many continued to do so as night settled over them. Until every wounded man had been seen to, Kiefer ordered, he did not want to leave the bridge for his own comfort or medical attention.

Look, he told himself, I've been beaten and battered before and fought on. Even as he leaned against anything solid to keep from collapsing, he told himself that old Captain Dixie was indestructible—just like his huge flat top. He wanted Dixie's boys to see with their own eyes that their skipper was not going to ask them to do anything he was not willing to do himself. That he was going to see this thing through, just as he expected every one of them to do. That he would not retire to sick bay until every single wounded man on the ship had been seen to.

And that is exactly what he did. Until almost midnight. Nearly twelve hours after the first attack on his ship, despite his serious wounds and loss of blood. No matter the useless right arm.

Only then, when someone reported that every injured man had now received medical attention, did Dixie Kiefer allow two corpsmen to lay him down on a stretcher and haul him down to sick bay.

CHAPTER FIFTEEN

Long, Slow Trip to Ulithi

TADASHI NAKAJIMA, THE COMMANDER OF THE JAPANESE KAMIKAZE AIR base on Formosa, later wrote, "Escort planes of the first and third sections [of the Niitaka suicide unit] returned shortly to base . . . with reports that direct hits had been scored on enemy carriers. One of the targets successfully attacked was identified as the American carrier *Ticonderoga*."

The US Navy's own initial report on the incident was just as succinct: "The *Ticonderoga* (CV-14) was damaged this date by suicide planes in position at lat. 22 [degrees] 40' N, long. 122 [degrees] 57' E. Also damaged by suicide planes this date were the light carrier *Langley* (CVL-27) . . . and the destroyer *Maddox* (DD-731)."

(Like the *Ticonderoga*, *Maddox* was struck by a kamikaze Zero, hit near her wardroom in the sudden attack. One officer and seven sailors were killed while eleven more were seriously injured. It would require more than two months in Ulithi for the destroyer to be repaired and returned to the war.)

Tokyo Rose actually gave more details about *Ticonderoga* in her gleeful report the night of January 21, even if she did have one key fact wrong. Officers gathered that night in the carrier's wardroom to listen to the usual broadcast. Servicemen truly enjoyed the music played during Rose's programs, but they alternately found her updates humorous or infuriating. That night, they were anxious to hear whether she mentioned the day's events. She had told the world the previous night that *Ticonderoga* had just passed from the South China Sea, south of Formosa, but would soon be encountering the might and will of the Imperial Japanese Navy.

The propagandist had often made such predictions before, and they had proven to be no more than wishful thinking on her part. Then, there she was, talking about their ship.

"I pass along my deepest sympathies to the families of the crew of the USS *Ticonderoga*," she cooed as the music faded away. "The *Essex*-class aircraft carrier is now at the bottom of the Pacific Ocean."

The officers who were gathered there in the wardroom laughed, though only for a moment. No, Big T had proven herself, and she remained very much afloat.

But then the mirth faded away. They had lost many shipmates that day. Many more lay wounded. Though most of those who had gone into the water had been rescued, there were more who were still missing and presumed lost.

The final official tally would be 143 men killed, 202 injured.

2224. Increased speed to 25 knots and took departure for Ulithi, Caroline Islands, in execution of orders of Commander Task Group 38.3.

The next day, during a long, escorted return to Ulithi, burials of the dead crewmembers began at the stern of the ship, on the hangar deck. Father and Lieutenant Cornelius O'Brien, chaplain and a Catholic priest, along with a Jewish crewmember, officiated, saying a prayer and speaking a few words as each man was sent into the sea.

Despite the losses and the sad ceremonies, everyone aboard Big T knew that it could have been much worse.

Doctor and Lieutenant F. E. Willing of the ship's medical department later summed up the feelings of just about everybody on *Ticonderoga*.

"I sincerely believe that had it not been for the fierce loyalty that Captain Dixie Kiefer had bred by friendly—almost fatherly—leadership, and his instantaneous command to flood the empty port gasoline tanks, the Big T would have been lost," Willing wrote. "His order to flood the tanks made the ship list to port. This forced the burning gasoline on the hangar deck to cascade over the side into the sea. Then his plea over the intercom to get the burning bomb- and rocket-laden planes off the

Men killed in kamikaze attacks are buried at sea.

hangar deck was enough to spur so many men to brave the flames and smoke that not a single bomb or rocket of our own exploded on the ship."

The navy would later confirm Willing's assessment, which was also the opinion of most—but not all—of the rest of the crew. And not only about Dixie Kiefer but also Executive Officer William Burch.

In the citation accompanying Burch's third Navy Cross—his previous two had come as a pilot when he had previously served with Dixie Kiefer on *Yorktown*, in addition to receiving a Distinguished Flying Cross for action earlier in the war—he was praised for "extraordinary heroism and distinguished service in the line of his profession as Executive Officer of the Aircraft Carrier U.S.S. TICONDEROGA (CV-14), when that ship was hit by an enemy Kamikaze airplane while deployed off Formosa, on 21 January 1945. Organizing fire-fighting crews on the hangar deck after his ship had been hit, Burch was the first to take a hose into the fire despite the billowing flames and continuous ammunition explosions although his clothes caught fire on two occasions. After the fire-fighting crews were functioning, he made his way to secondary control and manned his exposed battle station until severely wounded by shrapnel. Refusing to go to Sick Bay, he gave orders to be carried to the flight deck where he directed the fire fighting until the flames were under control."

Burch would go on, continuing a long navy career and eventually reaching the rank of rear admiral, though he never fully recovered from his injuries. Bits of shrapnel continued to work their way out of his skin, and he suffered from those wounds for the rest of his life. Burch died on January 21, 1989, the forty-fourth anniversary of the kamikaze attack on *Ticonderoga*, and is buried in Virginia Beach, Virginia.

Dixie Kiefer received the Silver Star "for conspicuous gallantry and intrepidity in action against the enemy while serving as Commanding Officer of the Aircraft Carrier U.S.S. TICONDEROGA (CV-14). Captain Kiefer skillfully and courageously fought his ship in such manner as to contribute greatly to decisive victories over the enemy in the far western Pacific. On 21 January 1945 when his ship was severely damaged by enemy air attack, in spite of serious wounds, he remained on the bridge and continued to direct operations until his ship was out of danger from enemy action. His unfaltering determination and exceptional leadership inspired his officers and crew to perform out-standingly throughout these operations."

In awarding Kiefer the Silver Star, then secretary of the navy James Forrestal—a former naval aviator himself—referred to Dixie Kiefer as "the indestructible man." It was a nickname Kiefer liked immensely, and he proudly referenced it and its source for the rest of his life.

There had been a running joke on *Ticonderoga* that the ship's compass followed their skipper anytime he went for a walk on the ship's deck. That was because he had so much metal in his body from his previous injuries. Joke or not, the skipper's resilience was an inspiration to his crew, especially after what happened out there off Formosa in January 1945.

However, in the days immediately following the attacks on *Ticond- eroga*, Captain Dixie did not feel like such a hero, nor did he feel especially indestructible. He was in a great deal of pain and was dangerously weakened by blood loss and complications from his broken arm. Besides that, he mourned the loss of each man who had been killed on his watch. He replayed over and over in his mind the many fateful decisions he had made before, during, and after the two brutal, mad crashes into his ship.

However, when he looked into the faces of the men in sick bay, and then later, as he was being carried on a stretcher to be transferred over to a hospital ship, the USS *Samaritan* (AH-10), he saw that none of them blamed him for what had happened. They were instead upset that their beloved skipper was leaving them and would no longer be in command. They truly loved this man and would miss "Captain Dixie" when he was gone.

Before being hauled over to the hospital ship, Kiefer motioned for his stretcher to be lifted up so he was almost vertical, practically standing. Then he took a moment to speak into a microphone, his voice carrying on the address system throughout all the decks of his beloved but wounded flat top, right past all the destruction where men still worked, still looked for more of the bodies of their shipmates.

"Well, gang, this is the last time I'll speak to you. I have tears in my eyes, and it isn't because I am hurt. I always did know that you were a damn good peacetime crew, and the other day out there, you proved to me that you were the best damn wartime crew in the Navy." He paused, partly from emotion, partly because he was still weak from losing all that blood up there on Big T's bridge. He swallowed hard and went on: "I did not leave the bridge until 11:30 that night, but afterwards, seeing how you men kept fighting back, I realized that I could do more good alive when I am able to come back out here again. I want to thank you men for saving the ship, which I thought was beyond saving. I'm going back to the States soon, and I'll be on the dock when you come in. The captain who takes my place will treat you like I did. Keep up your good work. The Big T still is and always will be the best damned ship in the Navy."

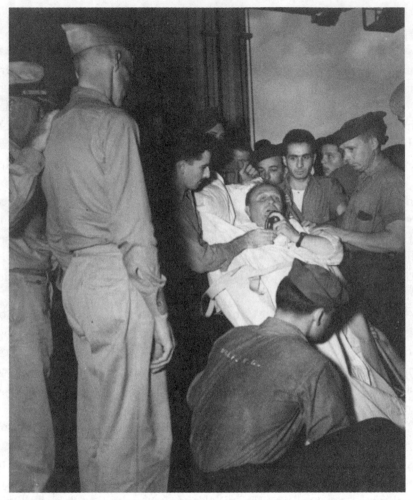

Captain Dixie speaks to his crew from his stretcher as he is transferred off his carrier to a hospital ship.

Mighty and sincere cheers rang out up and down the length of the wounded vessel. Men over on the hospital ship thought it sounded as if President Roosevelt or General MacArthur might have been shipping over. But it was just Captain Dixie, already thinking about getting back into the war after he had had time once again to heal from his latest collection of broken bones.

Crewmen salute as Dixie Kiefer is lifted over to the hospital ship.

As occurs any time there is major damage and casualties, an investigation started almost immediately to look into the *Ticonderoga* episode. Several crewmembers, including Kiefer and Burch, were questioned extensively about the events, their decisions, and precisely what happened out there, especially in the few hours before and after the attacks. Such inquiries are not necessarily to place blame or look for negligence; just as with the inspection of damage when the ship arrived at Bremerton, Washington, for repairs, they are a means of finding better ways to do things and to build warships to make them safer and more effective.

Even though the crew—officers and enlisted men alike—almost unanimously loved their skipper and felt he had done miraculous things to save the ship, not everyone agreed. One officer in particular would later be asked by staff members at Pacific Command about two very specific aspects of the incident.

Their concerns were about why *Ticonderoga* was not already under general quarters (antiaircraft), or at least GQ (damage control), before the first kamikaze attack. And they wanted to know why the captain and executive officer as well as other top officers were operating in the open-air bridge when the second plane struck, not at their proper assigned battle stations.

Usual procedure was to always bring the ship to general quarters anytime aircraft were returning from a mission and to remain so until the last airplane and crew had been recovered. Only then could they relax when it was determined that there were no Japanese planes tailing them. This was because the Japanese often followed carrier-based aircraft back to their ships to launch an attack of their own. Earlier that morning, one of the officers on the bridge had pointedly asked Captain Kiefer why he was standing down from GQ when planes were on their way back from Formosa.

"The men have worked hard," Captain Dixie had replied. "I want them to all have a good noon meal."

Kiefer also remained on the open-air bridge rather than the more heavily fortified pilothouse, or forward con, because he wanted to be closer to his men—to be better able to see what was going on, how his crew was responding, and to have the ability to shout orders or encouragement to his men on the deck below.

Nothing ever came of the questions asked about Dixie Kiefer and how he handled the ship that long, horrible day. Some believe it was because the captain was injured and probably would never be available to helm a ship again. Any kind of censure or even a serious inquiry would have only served to destroy morale on *Ticonderoga*. As noted, the crew loved Captain Dixie. They were, almost to a man, inspired by his actions and demeanor.

Still, a few believed that these were the reasons the carrier and her crew never received an award for that action. They also contend that this is one reason Dixie Kiefer has never been awarded his country's highest medal for bravery, the Medal of Honor, despite his remarkable efforts and conspicuous valor that day.

Also, as with any such deadly, high-stress event as this one, there are differing stories about who did what and when. We can rely on the consensus opinions from those who were there that day, though, and be reasonably sure that Kiefer did exactly what the Silver Star citation (and a later one that was even more detailed and included his performance during previous action in the Philippine campaign) said he did. And that he likely saved the ship and the lives of many more men.

We also have a confidential memo from the task force commander, Admiral Frederick C. Sherman, submitted in support of any potential award for valor to Dixie Kiefer. Sherman wrote, "Captain Kiefer exhibited qualities of leadership, courage, determination, and aggressiviness [*sic*] far above the average to be expected under similar conditions. It was due to his leadership that the damage to the TICONDEROGA was confined to fire damage on the hangar deck and the ship was able to proceed with full engineering power available to a base for repairs to battle damage."

But that was not all. Admiral Sherman also felt the need to expound on what many who served with Kiefer considered his primary strength, though it would have had no bearing on the awarding of any medal.

"Captain Kiefer, as Commanding Officer of the USS TICOND-EROGA, developed an unusually good organization on his ship and in his air group with particularly high morale in a very short space of time," Sherman stated. "He is an exceptionally able officer whom I would be glad to have under my command at any time."

What we do know for certain is that Kiefer was badly wounded, that he showed not only remarkable courage but also unbelievable resilience and strength, and that he was off to spend considerable time recuperating in several navy hospitals.

Dixie would soon learn, as he had fully expected, that the doctors would recommend he "be ordered to limited duty within the continental limits of the United States."

He did not know in January 1945 that the war would soon be over. A truce would come first in Europe, just after Dixie was discharged from the hospital in April. And then, thanks to the atomic bomb, hostilities with Japan would end abruptly, much sooner than anyone without knowledge of the bomb could have imagined. That would be in August, three months after Kiefer had begun a new shore assignment. Peace arrived before he could even be considered for command of another navy ship.

Dixie had done his job and done it well. Now, as he turned forty-nine years old, he was in a position to enjoy some of the benefits of his thirty years of service to his country. Another big plus? This time, his mother and sister would be able to follow him.

Chapter Sixteen

Quonset

DIXIE KIEFER GOT BACK TO HAWAII WELL AHEAD OF HIS SHIP. BIG T put into Ulithi for initial repairs to get her ready for the long run all the way to Bremerton, Washington, destined for some major work. Meanwhile, Dixie's hospital ship headed directly to Pearl Harbor with its load of injured crewmen from all three vessels that were hit on January 21.

Once he had made his good-bye speech and was out of sick bay on *Ticonderoga* and on the hospital ship *Samaritan*, surgeons immediately went to work on the captain's fractured arm. His medical report said, "[D]ebridement and medical reduction of fracture with pin fixation was performed." That meant dead and possibly infected tissue was removed, the bones in his arm—both the radius and the ulna were cleanly broken—were realigned, and pins were screwed in to hold them in place while they hopefully healed properly.

In Hawaii, Kiefer was transferred from the *Samaritan* to the navy hospital in Aiea Heights on February 3, "for treatment." The pins came out on March 2. Next, he made the long transfer to another naval hospital, this one in Quantico, Virginia, arriving on April 1. A week later he moved again, this time just up the road to Bethesda, Maryland, where he would ultimately be discharged on April 19.

Along with healing, Dixie Kiefer also began preparing for his new duty. He received a promotion, from captain to commodore, a naval rank that had not existed in the United States for almost fifty years. The US Navy had grown so tremendously during the war that there was concern there would be a large number of deserving officers at the rank of captain, good men who were holding high-responsibility commands and were in line to be promoted to the rank of rear admiral and to receive the pay increase that went with it. However, when peace ultimately came, there simply would be no need for that many admirals.

Those at the highest level of the US Navy came up with a solution: They could bring back the rank of commodore for those men, even though it had not been offered since 1899. President Roosevelt and Secretary Forrestal agreed. In May 1945, Dixie was a beneficiary of their decision and became Commodore Dixie Kiefer—with a pay raise—just as he was beginning his new duties.

However, even with the promotion and the orders to proceed to the Naval Air Station at Quonset Point, Rhode Island, to serve as the base's commanding officer, Dixie had to submit to yet another physical exam as part of his assumption of command. That assessment mentioned "multiple scars right side of body," a right arm—once the plaster cast was cut off and before a new one went on—that "showed wounds closed by their scar tissue," and that the use of his right wrist and hand was at least somewhat limited. X-rays of the bone fractures confirmed that healing was continuing, though not perfectly.

The doctors' report also cryptically mentions evidence of several other wounds and breaks, including his left arm and right leg and ankle. Considering his age, those would be left alone. Consulting surgeons suggested, however, that Dixie might need further work at some point on his most recent fractures. That bothersome cast on his right arm would be with him for a while longer.

Again, the medical board recommended that Dixie "be ordered to limited duty within the continental limits of the United States in an assignment not requiring full use of the right arm." So far as anyone could determine, he could manage to run a naval air base with limited use of an arm that was still in a cast. Dixie Kiefer was told that he could go ahead as ordered and take command of Quonset Point Naval Air Station. Within two weeks, the navy would add more responsibility, making him commander for all bases in the First Naval District, which included Maine, Vermont, New Hampshire, Massachusetts, and Rhode Island. Again, it was no problem that he had only limited use of his right arm.

Quonset Point Naval Air Station, Rhode Island.

Though the limb was still encased in plaster of Paris and hurt like hell, Dixie Kiefer proudly took charge and moved into the commanding officer's residence, in Quarters "A," at Point NAS, located on the west side of Narragansett Bay, just down from Providence and northwest of Newport. So did his mother, Tina, and sister, Honey. Both women remained unmarried. Another sister, who was married, lived in New York City, not that far away. Even though his brother and other sister, also both married, lived in California and Utah, respectively, Dixie considered the family back together again. At least all of them were now on the same continent. And though he was not commanding an aircraft carrier any longer, he was happy that his injuries had not ended his ability to offer valuable service to his country.

Quonset Point was the birthplace of the US Navy, going all the way back to the Revolutionary War, when a guard was placed there to watch for British warships that might sail up Narragansett Bay to raid coastal Rhode Island cities. Quonset Point NAS was established in July 1941 and had been a major facility throughout the war thus far. A certain young navy officer named Richard M. Nixon had gone through his basic officer training there in 1943. The distinctively shaped galvanized steel building, the Quonset hut, was first manufactured for military use at the Construction Battalion ("Seabee") headquarters there, beginning in 1941.

Quonset came from the Algonquian Indian language, and the area was so named by its earliest known human inhabitants. It is believed to mean, roughly, "a small, long place." That pretty much described the original point that jutted out into Narragansett Bay before the navy and the Seabees got to work. Much of the land mass where the base runways would be constructed came from dredging operations to create a harbor and a turning basin deep enough for aircraft carriers to be based there. Even more came from hills in the area that were knocked down to level the topography for aircraft landings and takeoffs. When the base opened, it had become much larger than when the Algonquians named it, and it now had a distinctive triangular shape.

As he settled into his new responsibilities at Quonset Point, Dixie Kiefer still missed being at sea, manning a ship with the complexity of an aircraft carrier. But most of all he missed the camaraderie with his men, regardless of their rank, background, or ethnicity.

Dixie continued to keep track of *Ticonderoga* and her crew. In Ulithi, the ship's air group was transferred over to USS *Hancock*, ironically the carrier that had originally borne the name *Ticonderoga* before insurance-company money led to the switch.

After a brief stop in Pearl Harbor, Big T steamed on to Puget Sound Naval Shipyard for extensive repairs. She was back to work in May, just as her former skipper was, in his new assignment. By June, the repaired carrier was providing air support for operations on Okinawa. Along the way, she once again encountered a strong typhoon and determined kamikazes, but only experienced relatively minor damage from the storm, and none from the Japanese. In July and August, planes off her decks sank a long list of battleships, carriers, and cruisers and struck key targets on the Japanese Home Islands, including in Tokyo. Her pilots were returning from a successful raid on Tokyo when word came that the Japanese had finally capitulated in the aftermath of Hiroshima and Nagasaki.

When the war ended, *Ticonderoga*'s aircraft continued to patrol on a full war-footing basis for several weeks. She spent most of that time seeking out and dropping supplies to known prisoner-of-war camps. She steamed into Tokyo Bay on September 16, four days after the peace treaty was signed there on the deck of USS *Missouri* (BB-63).

Ticonderoga would continue a long, storied history, throughout the Cold War and Vietnam and into the Space Age. She underwent several major modifications to keep her current and useful; was the floating home to thousands of officers, sailors, pilots, and other flying crewmen; received numerous citations and awards for service; and even recovered the Apollo 16 lunar mission landing capsule and astronauts off American Samoa in April 1972.

She was finally decommissioned on September 1, 1973, and sold for scrap two years later. Big T certainly gave American taxpayers their money's worth after Dixie Kiefer put her into commission and prepared her first crew. She and her men proudly served their country for almost thirty years.

For his part, Captain Dixie quickly settled into the relatively quiet duty involved with running the Quonset base and overseeing the business of his naval region. When he first took command, Kiefer not so jokingly told the officers on his staff, including his executive officer, Commander John Workman, to "go on doing your jobs and call me if you need me." They took him at his word; they were well aware their new commander was not only available if his attention was required but also keeping a sharp eye on everything to ensure it was being done properly.

Dixie Kiefer had not retired when he came to Rhode Island. He was still serving his country. He was on the job. And the job was important, even if he was not sending aircraft off on crucial missions or zigzagging his big carrier, dodging suicide attackers. This importance was not diminished in his mind, even when the Pacific War came to an end in August 1945.

He had now served his country in two world wars and lived to tell about it.

Just as had been the case on every ship or during every shore duty throughout his career, Kiefer was very popular with those with whom he served, officers and enlisted men alike. Enlisted women, too. There was a sizable contingent of WAVES (Women Accepted for Volunteer Emergency Service) based at Quonset. Dixie made it a point to stop by and deliver treats to the WAVES—flowers freshly picked from the garden he and his mother and sister had planted next to his quarters, and, during the summer, baskets of fresh vegetables or fruit he acquired from area farmers.

The *Yorktown* Cocktail Club was revived, too, but in a slightly different form. He scheduled regular clambakes on the beach. Skating parties, too. Several places in the bay were marked off and designated as swim areas for base personnel. He organized socials for sailors and WAVES with live music and dancing. He built up a small armada of new sailboats that could be reserved and enjoyed by all those who wanted to skim along on the bay waters or out into Long Island Sound. Commodore Dixie's steak breakfasts, over which he personally presided, quickly became legendary. He even procured more than 150 shotguns and set up a system in which sailors could check them out and go hunting in their spare time.

A hallmark of practically all of Kiefer's social activities was that enlisted men and officers had equal status. Rank was left at the door, beach, or dock.

One sailor later said, "Because of Commodore Kiefer's efforts on our behalf, it became more fun to remain on the station at night and on weekends for recreation than it was to go off on liberty passes."

As he had throughout his navy career, Dixie continued to praise the enlisted men and to give them credit for the success the navy had earned in World War II. As he was in the process of assuming command at Quonset Point, he was a guest at a press function at the Waldorf Astoria Hotel in Manhattan. Someone inquired about his injuries, pointing to the cast on his arm and asking him whether he considered himself a hero.

"The real heroes are the servicemen who did not have the benefit of attending the Naval Academy," Kiefer said. "The ones who have not benefited from thirty years of steady employment and good pay as I have. No, the heroes are the reservists and the greenhorn sailors."

Kiefer went on to specifically mention the service of African American sailors who were mostly relegated to serving as mess workers and stewards.

"There is nothing heroic about us 'regulars,'" he concluded. "We aren't giving up homes, good jobs, and pleasant shores to go to sea."

In late October or early November, Dixie endured yet another operation on his bad right arm. This meant he would have to continue wearing the awkward cast, which got in the way of everything from personal hygiene to signing his name. It also meant he could not yet be re-certified as physically able to pilot an airplane.

In truth, as commodore, he had plenty of excellent pilots at his beck and call, and though he had to go through all the paperwork to requisition and justify the use of an airplane for his frequent travels, he had several planes that offered comfortable and safe transportation anytime he needed it. This included a Beechcraft "Twin Beech" JRB-4 Expeditor. He could even round up several hitchhikers to ride with him on that bird, since it allowed for up to six passengers in addition to its two pilots.

There were always men who needed a lift to visit family or just for a nice weekend liberty when Dixie made out-of-town trips. Why let those empty seats go to waste? Sure, the men could take the train or stick out a thumb, but why squander precious time getting to and from home when Commodore Dixie could offer them a ride on his plane? And he always made the offer to anyone, regardless of rank or station in life.

Still, Dixie would have liked to be able to fly solo, to take the stick and once again soar and knock holes in the clouds, just as he had done off and on since June 1922.

In November, Kiefer received an invitation to come down to New York City for a meeting with an old friend, an aviation executive. The man wanted to discuss having Dixie give a talk to some of his company's aircraft workers, to tell them just what a major role they had played in their country's victory over the Nazis and the Japanese. He had other aircraft business he wanted to talk over with Kiefer as well. There might even be discussion of a possible peacetime job if Dixie decided to retire from the navy.

There was one other incentive to make the trip: The man just happened to have tickets to the college gridiron showdown between Army and Notre Dame at Yankee Stadium on Saturday, November 10. Both teams were undefeated. Army was ranked number one in the country. Notre Dame was number two. This was to be the college football game of the year so far.

Now Kiefer was a navy man through and through, and his team was having an especially good year. They would end the 1945 season ranked number three in the country by the Associated Press. Even so, the old high school football player from Nebraska could not turn down the chance to see in person the nation's two top-ranked teams go to war. And to watch in person the army's amazing player, Doc Blanchard, the man everyone was picking to win the Heisman Trophy that year.

Kiefer enthusiastically accepted his friend's invitation. He then checked the schedule to see who might be able to pilot and co-pilot the Beechcraft on the short flight down to New York on Saturday and then back home on Sunday. It was only about 160 miles each way, about an hour of flying on each leg of the trip.

He got his assistant busy with the obligatory red-tape paperwork. He told his mother and sister he would be out of town Saturday night. He made it known around the base that the plane would be going that way, and when. Then he stood by to see who else wanted to ride along, even though it was relatively late notice and would be a very quick trip.

Three men—an officer and two enlisted men—promptly took Commodore Dixie up on his kind offer of a lift down to New York City.

And, of course, a ride back home again on Sunday.

Chapter Seventeen

"Over the Northerly Portion of the City of Beacon"

DIXIE KIEFER LIKED HAVING LIEUTENANT LLOYD HEINZEN AS HIS pilot when he traveled, and not simply because Heinzen was of relatively recent German descent, as was Kiefer. It was more likely because the man was a genuine war hero, a true "ace" who had earned two Distinguished Flying Crosses for his carrier-based action during the war. If Heinzen could skirmish with Japanese Zeroes and fly cover over enemy ships and bases, he could certainly haul Commodore Dixie all around the country while he traveled on official business. Fortunately, Heinzen was available for the New York trip.

So was a skilled co-pilot, Lieutenant Hans Karl Kohler, though Dixie had not yet gotten to know the young man. But again, Kohler was chosen as a member of the flight crew not because he was of German extraction, which he was—born in Germany, he had come to the States when he was just three years old—but because Kohler, too, happened to be an experienced pilot with notable service against the enemy. He had only been back in the States for three weeks from duty in the South Pacific and was slated to receive a Distinguished Flying Cross for sinking a Japanese freighter. Kohler was a veteran of twenty missions against enemy targets and had only reported for duty at Quonset Point on October 28.

Dixie Kiefer also knew the two young fliers—Heinzen was twenty-seven, and Kohler only twenty-five, and neither was married—would likely enjoy a weekend in Manhattan. Kohler even had family nearby

A Beechcraft Expeditor similar to the one used by Dixie Kiefer for the trip to New York City, November 1945.

in Garfield, New Jersey, only a few miles from their destination airport in Caldwell.

When the commodore's Beechcraft Expeditor lifted off the runway at Quonset Point early on the morning of November 10—just after inspection by Kiefer of the marine contingent based there—they had three additional passengers aboard. This included a fourth officer, Lieutenant Commander Ignatius Zielinski, and two enlisted men, Aviation Machinist's Mate Clarence Hooper and Seaman First Class David Wood.

Zielinski was the Quonset base's assistant medical officer and an experienced physician, having worked at both the Mayo Clinic and Johns Hopkins Hospital. He was forty-five and would also be attending the football game with Kiefer. Hooper was twenty-two, and Wood was twenty-three. Hooper, an African American, was the only one on the plane that day who was married. But just barely. His wife of one week lived in Greensboro, North Carolina.

As expected, it was a relatively quick and uneventful flight across Connecticut and the northern New York City borough of the Bronx to the landing field at what is today Essex County International Airport. The airport is located near Caldwell, New Jersey, about twenty miles west of New York City, and was then formally known as Curtis (Caldwell) Wright Airport, so named for aviation pioneers the Wright brothers, just as one of the early ships on which Dixie Kiefer served had been.

Once on the ground, Dr. Zielinski and Commodore Dixie joined up with Kiefer's friend to get over to Yankee Stadium for the football game. Everyone was excited about being in the stands at the historic ballpark for such a momentous confrontation. The rest of the men scattered to their various pursuits.

We do not know whether Kiefer was aware that the airport where he landed was in Essex County, yet another coincidence in this story. Dixie's former ship was an Essex-class aircraft carrier, and the USS Essex was a sister ship that was in the same task force as Ticonderoga.

Still another coincidence: Dr. and Commander Ignatius Zielinski had once served as the county medical examiner in his hometown of Salem, Massachusetts. Salem is in (and Zielinski was the employee of) Essex County, Massachusetts.

The Caldwell, New Jersey, airport is today best known as the place from which John F. Kennedy Jr. took off for his ill-fated flight in July 1999. That crash claimed not only JFK Jr.'s life but also the lives of his wife and sister-in-law. This flight ended in Long Island Sound off the island of Martha's Vineyard, not very far from Quonset Point.

The Army–Notre Dame game was likely the highlight of Dixie Kiefer's weekend, even though the outcome was hardly as thrilling as the press's buildup for the showdown had promised. Army easily won the game, 48–0. The Black Knights' two star players, Doc Blanchard ("Mr. Inside") and Glen Davis ("Mr. Outside"), dazzled the crowd at Yankee Stadium that day, as well as flummoxing the Fighting Irish. Davis scored three touchdowns. Blanchard had two.

Despite the rivalry between the service academies, Dixie Kiefer was glad a military school had won. He also knew that the Army victory over the Fighting Irish made the upcoming rivalry game with his Midshipmen of Navy an even more monstrous event. But mostly he just enjoyed the atmosphere and the company of his friends, including a nice dinner in a Manhattan restaurant that evening.

Three weeks later, on December 1, Army and Navy played before 102,000 people, including President Harry Truman, at Philadelphia. Though Navy would put up a gallant fight, Army won the game 32–13. Because of the recent end to the war and the Associated Press rankings of the two teams involved, many still consider the 1945 face-off between Army and Navy the greatest service academy game in the long history of the rivalry. Doc Blanchard was awarded the Heisman Trophy for 1945. Glen Davis would go on to be the 1946 recipient even as Blanchard continued his military career in another "game" in which he excelled—as a fighter pilot.

Kiefer and his pilots and passengers had agreed to assemble about mid-morning of November 11 back at Caldwell Wright Airport so they could return to the base. It was Armistice Day, after all. This was the day set aside to commemorate the signing of the treaty that ended the Great War (World War I). The signing ceremony had been held at the eleventh hour of the eleventh day of the eleventh month in 1918.

They had every reason to believe that they would be home in plenty of time for a late lunch. We do not know whether any of them planned to attend formal Armistice Day activities, but that might well have been the case. With their aircraft's top speed of 225 miles per hour, it should have taken them just over an hour to get home, assuming there were no weather issues along the way.

With Heinzen and Kohler at the controls, the Beechcraft Expeditor revved its twin engines while the pilots checked gauges and systems, preparing for takeoff. It was just before 11:00 a.m., Eastern Standard Time. Kiefer, Zielinski, Hooper, and Wood all climbed aboard and buckled up as they discussed what each had done the evening before. There was, of course, plenty of talk about the previous day's football game and speculation about how the Midshipmen would fare against the Black Knights. The winner would likely be the Associated Press national champs. There was no feeling of officers versus enlisted men, white and black, on board the plane. It was simply a half dozen friends headed back home after a pleasant weekend trip.

A later inquiry by the navy gave cold, clinical details of what would transpire over the next hour of that quiet Sunday morning.

> On 11 November 1945, at or about 10:45 a.m., Lt. Heinzen, through the Traffic Controller at Caldwell-Wright, duly requested of ATC New York an instrument flight requirements clearance for a flight by subject aircraft from Caldwell-Wright to Quonset Point.

It is likely that Beechcraft #44632 lifted off the runway at Caldwell at just about the eleventh hour of the eleventh day of the eleventh month. Heinzen first pointed the aircraft to the northwest, to avoid all the congestion around New York City. Then, based on instructions from Air Traffic Control (ATC), they climbed gently and headed north. They were aiming for an altitude of a little better than 3,000 feet before finally pointing the plane's nose east-northeast, paralleling the Hudson River and ultimately turning for a direct course back toward Rhode Island.

> At 11:33 a.m. ATC New York requested position and altitude of aircraft and directed pilot to stand by for instructions. At 11:38 a.m. the aircraft requested of Stewart Radio permission to descend and cruise in accordance with Contact Flight Rules to Quonset Point.

For some reason, Lloyd Heinzen was asking flight controllers to allow him to fly at a relatively low altitude using landmarks and geography he could see on the ground along the way to navigate home rather than rely on his airplane's instruments, as John F. Kennedy Jr. would later do on his doomed flight. The initial primary landmark for Heinzen would have been the Hudson River. At this point, he was speaking by

Mount Beacon, New York, looking southwest with Hudson River on the right. (Photo by David Rocco)

radio with controllers at Stewart Airport near Newburgh, New York, just across the Hudson from Beacon.

> Stewart Radio answered and directed aircraft to stand by for instructions, then to cruise and cross Stewart Radio at an altitude of 3,000 feet. At 11:40 a.m. aircraft acknowledged the last communication, stated it would proceed to Stewart and asked to descend over Stewart to cruise.

A routine flight so far. Not a bad day. The plane was apparently performing perfectly. The men behind the pilot and co-pilot—officers and enlisted men, black and white—were chatting, enjoying the ride.

At 11:43 a.m. aircraft acknowledged weather communication. Aircraft asked to make descent and was acknowledged to wait for permission to make descent.

Air Traffic Control at Stewart/Newburgh had alerted Heinzen that there might be weather issues ahead. Heinzen, though still southwest of Newburgh and Beacon, could already see on the horizon the weather the airport was talking about. There were some clouds, all right, but nothing that looked too ominous. The experienced flier was likely not concerned. Lord knows he had zoomed through his share of low clouds and pea soup, lining up on targets, sometimes with a Japanese fighter on his ass. And he had repeatedly located and set down on his carrier in the middle of a big ocean while being pelted by a tropical rainstorm.

Now Heinzen merely wanted permission to fly a bit lower so he could maintain visible contact with the ground, see the Hudson River and other geographical features. Maybe, too, the series of beacon lights that had been placed on mountain peaks along the Hudson River for the purpose of guiding pilots through the same kind of conditions as the ones that occurred on November 11, 1945. That would help him to stay on course past the mountains that he likely knew lay to the north of where he wanted to turn eastward. The tallest thing around them was Mount Beacon, and it was much farther north of their intended course. Even so, at 1,600 feet tall, it was well below their cruising altitude.

As he awaited word from ATC, Lieutenant Heinzen eased the stick down just a bit. He was trying to stay just below the suddenly thickening clouds, the rain and fog, all to keep within sight of the earth below and remain on course for home.

At or about 11:57 a.m. the aircraft was sighted in flight over the northerly portion of the city of Beacon by at least three observers . . . flying through the base of the lower-hanging clouds.

Whether they realized it yet or not, the men aboard the Expeditor—including the indestructible Dixie Kiefer—were considerably north of where they thought they were.

And they were already in deep, deep trouble.

Chapter Eighteen

Quiet Sunday

[The aircraft's] altitude and flight attitude cannot be accurately determined. It was on an east-southeasterly course. When last seen, the aircraft disappeared into the clouds overhanging the western slope of Bald Hill. All such witnesses heard a crash occur within a very short interval after losing sight of the aircraft; the exact duration of such interval being impossible to determine as a fact.

It had been a quiet Sunday so far in the quaint, historic village of Beacon, New York. Church services were just concluding around town, worshippers emerging from sanctuaries into a drizzly, foggy midday. It was barely 40 degrees. A raw wind was blowing.

At 12:05 p.m., the phone rang on the desk of Sergeant Ralph Parker down at the Beacon Police Department. The caller identified himself as William Atkinson, from over on Washington Avenue.

"I just saw an airplane swoop down out of the clouds," Atkinson reported. "He was flying east. Then he disappeared into the clouds again, toward Mount Beacon. Then I heard a big noise. I think he may have crashed up there on the mountain."

Sergeant Parker thanked him and hung up, but before he could send anybody over to get details and check it out, the phone jangled again.

"This is David Frost . . . Depuyster Avenue. I just saw an airplane flying real low under the clouds, like he was looking for a place to land or maybe see a landmark. Then he went back into the clouds and I heard something that sounded like an explosion."

The quiet morning had suddenly become a harsh Sunday afternoon.

More calls came in, each excitedly talking about hearing and seeing the plane and then the sound of a crash somewhere in the direction of the twin mountains, maybe toward the town of Fishkill. Benjamin Ruf and Raymond Schultz were near the Fairview cemetery on Washington Avenue when they heard the roar of the plane's engines. They instinctively looked up.

"It was up about the height of two trees," Schultz reported.

It seemed everyone had lately become more attuned to low-flying aircraft. There had been another crash of a small navy plane only two weeks before, that one near Wingdale, which, like Beacon, was in Dutchess County. Two young fliers died there. Others remembered more crashes on the mountains, closer to Beacon and Fishkill, including the one back in 1935 that had killed two navy men, Lincoln Denton and Floyd Hart.

Off-duty Beacon police officers, New York state troopers, and Dutchess County sheriff's deputies quickly assembled to begin searching, to try to locate any plane crash that may have occurred, and to get to possible survivors—if any—as quickly as possible. Air Traffic Control from Stewart Airport confirmed there had been a navy plane flying through the area, that they had not been able to contact its pilot since about noon, and they were afraid it might have gotten lost in the weather.

The weather that had gotten progressively worse.

"The heavy fog and rain made the visibility impossible for more than 10 to 15 feet," the local newspaper later reported. "At 4:30 p.m. 25 Stewart Field soldiers commanded by Major Carpenter arrived on the scene. They searched through the mountainside until 6 p.m. when darkness halted operations."

By then, the navy had confirmed that one of their aircraft was hours overdue on a flight from Caldwell, New Jersey, back to Quonset Point Naval Air Station in Rhode Island. They also confirmed that one of the passengers on that plane was Commodore Dixie Kiefer, the commander of the base and a Pacific War hero. He was declared missing.

The names of the others on the plane were not released by the navy, pending officials contacting next of kin to let them know that they were overdue. Two PBY "flying boat" aircraft, a helicopter, and a navy blimp were all requisitioned. They were to show up first thing on Monday to try to help locate the downed plane, once there was daylight, and assuming the skies had cleared somewhat.

Sunday night, even as darkness fell and the drizzle and fog sank lower, state police did not give up. There could be injured men up there in need of medical help. They brought in giant searchlights and tried to illuminate the mountainside, but it was still dark and the vegetation was thick, almost impenetrable. Even so, a dozen more troopers showed up and began hacking their way toward where witnesses had reported hearing the crash.

The Providence *Evening Bulletin* would later report that Kiefer's plane was thirty miles off the usual course from Caldwell to Quonset Point, a regular route followed by navy aircraft, and one familiar to the aircraft's pilots. The paper also wrote of a remarkable impromptu volunteer effort by those stationed at Quonset Point: "A party of 200 officers, sailors and marines set out from Quonset shortly before one yesterday [Monday] morning with busses [*sic*], crash trucks and ambulances, loaded with wet weather gear and equipment for rescue work."

The volunteers' intent was to get to Beacon and help locate the crash wreckage in time to possibly save their beloved commander and any other of their "shipmates" they could. They prayed that the men had all managed to survive the impact on the mountainside. It is a measure of how much the base personnel loved and respected their boss that two hundred of them piled into buses and other vehicles in the middle of the night and raced across the twisting byways of Connecticut and New York to the Hudson Valley to try to find and help him.

"Two naval officers in a fast car preceded the party into Beacon, interviewed townspeople and fixed the precise location of the crash. With daybreak, the 200 volunteers from the command began the arduous task of clearing a way for 2,000 yards up the wooded slope to the wreckage. Progress was extremely slow, as the men, with axes or machetes, cleared brush and trees. After two hours' work, the party reached the wreckage near the summit of the mountain."

According to other press reports, another trio of searchers—Joseph Brown, his son Joseph Jr., and Charles Wood, all from the Beacon area—

had actually located the crash scene at about 2:30 on Monday morning, November 12.

Initial speculation by witnesses was that there had been explosions and fire, as if the plane might have been carrying some kind of ordnance. Some reported that it was the delayed igniting of flares in the wreckage early on Monday morning that finally led Wood and the Browns to the twisted wreckage. They were on a distant ridge when they suddenly heard the snapping and cracking of what might have been flares. They also saw flashes, even through the thick, swirling fog. That led them to work their way through the scrub in that direction.

At first, they hopefully believed that what they saw and heard might be survivors firing flares to get the attention of rescue parties. That, of course, proved not to be the case, but only after they had hacked their way through another two miles of underbrush to reach the source of the flashes. The flares had likely been set off by heat from a smoldering fire. Any explosion heard immediately after the crash might have been from the aircraft's fuel tanks. There were signs that there had been considerable fire. Most of the victims were badly burned.

The first to make it to the scene realized immediately that none of the victims had set off the flares. It was obvious all six had died instantly.

Once the wreckage was reached by others, police, the Quonset contingent, and more, they confirmed the crash as that of the navy's overdue Beechcraft Expeditor and that there were no survivors. The body of Dixie Kiefer was found about twenty-five feet from the crumpled wreckage of his plane, where he had been thrown upon the plane's impact with the immovable mountain. He had not been burned at all but died from the force of the crash. The men from Quonset Point identified him. The cast on his right arm made it obvious that this was "the man the Japanese could never kill," as some press reports had mentioned. To be sure, official papers found in Dixie's uniform pocket further confirmed the sad truth.

"[Kiefer's] gold-braided cap lay near the body," the *Evening Bulletin* reporter testified. "An enlisted man [from Quonset Point] picked it up and hung it on the broken root of a tree that had been knocked over by the plane. The commodore's wounded arm, still in a cast, was outstretched above his head, and the cast aided in positive identification of the hero's body."

Front page of the Poughkeepsie *New Yorker* newspaper on November 12, 1945. Because of his heroic career and movie appearance, Dixie Kiefer received most of the press coverage after the crash.

Some papers around the country ran a recent news photo of Kiefer signing the cast of another wounded naval officer while both were at the hospital at Bethesda. Brothers-in-arms, indeed.

The newspaper story goes on: "One body, that of a flight captain, was found in the broken fuselage. The body had been slightly burned."

A newspaper reporter wrote, "Their searchlights picked out the plane—or what was left of it. It had shed one motor. The fuselage was a crumpled mass. The bodies were scattered, hardly recognizable."

Other news reports quoted local fliers, speculating that the pilot of the transport had deliberately brought his plane to a lower altitude looking for landmarks for contact flying (navigating visually, without instrumentation) and that it had rammed into the side of the mountain at a speed of around 150 miles per hour. The damage at the crash site confirmed it was a direct plunge at high speed into the ground and thick undergrowth. There was no evidence that Heinzen had tried to pull up at the last instant. The airplane tore off treetops, split some trees in two, and scattered its parts and its passengers as far as four hundred feet from the spot where it hit.

As marines from Quonset Point loaded Commodore Kiefer's body onto a stretcher and began the long, arduous hike down the side of the mountain, they told bystanders how truly sad they and everyone at the base were about the tragedy. Kiefer had reviewed these same marines shortly before climbing into the plane and heading off to New York the previous Saturday morning. He had been his usual jovial self, correcting where needed, but doing so in a positive, uplifting manner.

The scene was eerily reminiscent of Kiefer being carried off *Ticonderoga* to be transferred to the hospital vessel. But this time, there would be no emotional farewell speech. Captain Dixie would not be waiting on the pier when "his ship" arrived.

How did those back at the base react to the confirmation of the worst? Someone described those there as numb, disbelieving. They, too, had been convinced that their commander was indestructible. Everyone knew his record, was aware of his various injuries, in wartime and peacetime. And that he had bounced back from every one of them to continue to lead in a spectacular and effective manner. He had survived all that the Germans and Japanese had thrown at him, only to be claimed in the fresh peacetime by a truly imperishable obstacle, one that was millions of years old.

Command of Quonset Point was taken over by Kiefer's XO, Commander John Workman. Responsibility for the bases in Dixie's naval area fell to his chief of staff, Captain Truman Penney.

Telephone operators confirmed that the base switchboards were jammed with calls. They came from both on and off the post, people throughout all levels of the navy or the general public, each trying to find out more information. Most were hoping against hope that there was a mistake. That Dixie had found a way to dodge this latest danger. Or that searchers would find Dixie alive, that he had once again cheated death and would have an even more amazing survival tale to spin at his next clambake or steak breakfast. Many urged that their sympathies be relayed to the commodore's mother and sister, who had become fixtures at Quonset in a very short time.

One of those calls came from a hospital in Brunswick, Maine, where Commander Joe Taylor, the Brunswick Naval Air Station commander and yet another war hero, was recuperating from major surgery. He wanted to get the latest news on his old friend. Only a few days before, Dixie Kiefer had visited Taylor in his hospital room, brightening his day, cheering him on.

Everyone at the Quonset Point base had a Commodore Dixie story to tell. Some remembered how he had joked about all of his injuries, lifting a pant leg or rolling up a sleeve to show scars. He told everyone that he still had one good limb that had not yet been broken in service to his country. It was his intention to go back into action and see whether he could fix that oversight.

"Too bad the war is over before I can let the enemy try one more time to get at old Dixie," he had said with a laugh, a twinkle in his eye.

Later, a reporter noted a bit of irony in this tragic crash. The spot where Commodore Dixie's plane went down was only a few miles from the birthplace of James Forrestal, the secretary of the navy, the man who had recently bestowed on Kiefer the Distinguished Service Cross, one of the nine medals he was awarded in his two-war career. And the man who had, as you might recall, conferred upon Kiefer the title "The Indestructible Man."

The US Navy's inevitable official inquiry into the crash summed up their findings succinctly:

Opinions: The proximate cause of the accident cannot be determined. The aforesaid deaths occurred in line of duty and were not the result of their own misconduct.

Now, with the crash located and the bodies of the victims recovered, it was a time for mourning, and for the proper burial of each.

CHAPTER NINETEEN

Arlington, Sec 3, Site 4072-C

We shall meet again with those we honor tonight and they will ask us if they died in vain. They fought for high and mighty and fine principles. They were willing to give up their lives. They gave everything they had. They were men among men in this world of injustice. They did not fight for personal gain or for national expansion. The principles for which they did fight and died will live with us.

THOSE WERE THE WORDS OF FATHER JOSEPH MADDEN, DELIVERED AT the Armistice Day services at Beacon's Memorial Building on the evening of Sunday, November 11, 1945. Even as they were being spoken, search parties continued to attempt to make their way up the tough, forbidding terrain of Mount Beacon, only a few miles away, seeking to reach the wreckage of Commodore Dixie Kiefer's airplane.

The powerful message, of course, was not specifically about Kiefer and his comrades, though it could certainly have applied. We can also assume that the plane crash on the nearby peak was very much on the minds of those attending the town's twenty-seventh observance of Armistice Day.

The next few weeks after the tragic accident were filled with tribute stories in the hometown newspapers of the crash victims and those in Rhode Island, as well as throughout the country. Dixie Kiefer's name—better known than those of the other victims—was typically the one mentioned in headlines, not only due to his well-documented heroism in two wars but also because of his prominent role in the Academy Award–winning documentary film *The Fighting Lady*.

With one exception, the other crash victims were also widely praised—not just by the media but also by those with whom they had served and by the awarding to several of them of posthumous medals and citations.

In Garfield, New Jersey, the local paper tracked down the brother of the Expeditor's co-pilot, Lieutenant Hans Kohler, for a comment. Rudolph Kohler, a twice-wounded army vet who had served in Europe, happened to be home on furlough when he and the family received word about what had occurred.

"Hans never talked much about his experiences," Rudolph Kohler said. "He never went in much for publicity or pictures."

Hans Kohler had gone to war as an enlisted man, a gunner's mate, before he transferred in 1943, went to Pensacola for flight training, and earned his commission as an officer. He held the Air Medal in recognition of valorous action against an enemy submarine and two more Gold Stars in lieu of additional Air Medals. He was to formally receive the Distinguished Flying Cross for his role in helping send an enemy ship to the bottom as part of Patrol Bombing Squadron 27. James Forrestal had signed the final draft of the citation (or at least an underling had stamped the navy secretary's name) less than a month before Kohler's death.

Hans Kohler's body was sent home to New Jersey for burial.

Reporters detailed the combat service in the Pacific of the plane's pilot, Lieutenant Lloyd Heinzen. During his eight months in combat there, he shot down eight Japanese planes, which qualified him as an "ace." He had been shot down himself but survived the crash, was rescued, and returned to the fray. He was already the recipient of a Distinguished Flying Cross and two Gold Stars in lieu of two more, plus many other citations and awards.

Heinzen was a native of Colorado Springs, Colorado. He was buried in Arlington National Cemetery in Washington, DC.

The Salem, Massachusetts, *Evening News* wrote of Lieutenant Commander Ignatius Zielinski, "[His] father died when he was a young fellow but determination and courage, which the doctor had so nobly displayed throughout his lifetime, carried him through school to an education." The paper noted that Zielinski had worked his way through Tufts Medical School, first as a clerk in a pharmacy, and then by becoming a licensed pharmacist.

David Wood was a Seaman First Class from North Franklin, Connecticut. Quonset Point NAS XO—and acting commander after Commodore Dixie's death—J. T. Workman wrote a letter to the families of each of the victims after the tragedy. In the message to Wood's father, Workman said, "I desire to express how deeply we feel his loss . . . his record had been commendable. His attention to duty and loyalty won praise from his superiors and affection and respect from his shipmates who sincerely mourn his loss. His friendship will remain a precious legacy to those of us who had the privilege of serving with him."

Among Wood's personal effects shipped home to his family were nine handkerchiefs, a pair of gym shoes, and a flatiron. His body was also shipped to his hometown for burial, escorted by Seaman First Class Wallace Wadyka.

The one Mount Beacon victim who was not the recipient of any awards, praise from his superiors, or lengthy articles in local papers was Clarence Hooper. He was also the only one who had been at Quonset Point for a while, since October 1943, after he had completed basic training at Great Lakes, Illinois. The newspaper in Clarence Hooper's hometown of Greensboro, North Carolina, described him in a short article as "the 22-year-old negro youth" who had died along with Commodore Dixie Kiefer "in the crash of a navy plane on Mt. Beacon, New Jersey [sic], Sunday." Hooper was survived by his mother, father, and brother, and by his wife, Doris Marie Hooper. They had married only eleven days prior to the deadly crash. Hooper had added "Doris Griffin Hooper" as his beneficiary on October 31. The couple had one child, Patsy Ann, who was thirteen months old at the time of his death. Hooper also had a son, Robert Lee Miles, from a prior relationship.

Hooper had voluntarily joined the Naval Reserve in Greensboro in July 1943. His service records indicate satisfactory service and test scores. It also appears that at one point, he had been approved for promotion to petty officer, which apparently never happened. He was also "ordered to duty involving flying this date" on the first day of each month, February, March, April, and June, and the 16th of July, all in 1945. However, next to each of those dates is another stamp, dated the 15th of each month—or July 31—with the notation "Orders to duty involving flying revoked this date." We have no record of the nature of "duty involving flying" for which Clarence Hooper may have been a candidate, whether it was as a pilot or some other type of flying crew. There is also no indication of why Hooper may have been approved for such duty and then denied it only two weeks later a total of five times.

However, at the top of the form on which these notes appear, someone has handwritten in large letters "NEGRO." It would be October 1948 before Jesse Leroy Brown became the navy's first African American aviator.

The authors will allow the reader to draw his or her own conclusion.

Another one of the interesting coincidences we have noted throughout this tale? Just like Dixie Kiefer, the man with whom he served and died, Clarence Hooper did not have a middle name. All service records have "(none)" in that field on the forms.

And yet another one: The maiden name of the mother of one of the authors of this book (Don Keith) was "Doris Griffin."

Hooper's body was returned to Greensboro for burial. The standard notification telegram sent to inform Doris Hooper of her husband's death promised, "If [the remains are] sent home, expenses for preparation, encasement, and transportation will be prepaid and funeral expenses not exceeding fifty dollars will be refunded on application to the Bureau of Medicine and Surgery X. Sincere sympathy is extended to you in your great loss."

The navy also awarded Mrs. Hooper $117 per month for six months as "death gratuity pay," for a total of $702.

There was a memorial service at Quonset Point on Thursday, November 15, three days after the crash, to honor the six "shipmates" lost on the mountain. The Quonset Choir sang "Abide with Me" and "The Navy Hymn (Strong to Save)." Soprano and WAVE Helen Clayton performed a rendition of "The Lord's Prayer."

A new version of "The Navy Hymn" had been adopted only five years earlier not only to include references to men in danger on the sea, as in the traditional version of the song that had come into use at the Naval Academy in 1879, but also to ask for mercy for those traveling on the ground and in the air.

One of the newly added verses sung by the choir that day at the memorial service was especially appropriate:

> O Spirit, whom the Father sent
> To spread abroad the firmament;
> O Wind of heaven, by thy might
> Save all who dare the eagle's flight,
> And keep them by thy watchful care
> From every peril in the air.

The next day, and only four days after Commodore Dixie's body was carried down the side of Mount Beacon, his remains arrived by train at Union Station in Washington, DC, at 8:15 a.m. Five family members were on that train as well. Funeral services and burial at Arlington National Cemetery were scheduled for 10:00 a.m. in section 3, site 4072-C, just off the cul de sac of Miles Drive. After the service, those family members would hurry back to Union Station and catch a train set to depart at 2:00 p.m.

In February 1946, the new all-denominational chapel at Quonset Point Naval Air Station was dedicated and named in memory of Dixie Kiefer. A prayer asked that Commodore Kiefer be "blessed with eternal happiness." In the ceremony, he was credited with being the one whose efforts "brought to fruition" the construction of the chapel for the princely sum of $75,000 (just over a million bucks in 2020 dollars). Its unique design featured four different altars that were rotatable so they could face either of two meeting areas. They represented Protestant, Catholic, Jewish, and nondenominational faiths.

There was another special ceremony at Quonset Point on Memorial Day, May 30, 1946. As part of the service, a memorial plaque to Commodore Kiefer was unveiled by Dixie's sister Phyllis (Honey). The event

Commodore Dixie Kiefer's tombstone at Arlington National Cemetery in Washington, DC.

began with a flyover by aircraft based at Quonset. One of the planes carried a wreath that was flown out to sea and dropped in memory of all men in the US Navy, Marine Corps, and Coast Guard who had "laid down their lives for our country."

A special rededication ceremony was held at the Dixie Kiefer Memorial Chapel in January 1955. The same litany that was read in the original dedication of the chapel nine years earlier was repeated at this event.

The US Navy closed Quonset Point Naval Air Station in 1975. With no more need for the chapel, plans were made to donate the building and move it to the Galilee Mission to Fishermen in Narragansett, Rhode Island. That idea was abandoned when it was discovered that the structure was rife with asbestos. The steeple, however, was fine and had been in storage at the Seabee base. It went to the mission, where plans were to erect it as a memorial to fishermen who had been lost at sea.

Back to November 1945, and to Commodore Dixie's burial at Arlington National Cemetery. A telegram was sent on November 13 from Quonset Point NAS to the Navy Bureau of Personnel, informing staff members of the arrival of Dixie's remains and family members, as well as other funeral details.

This telegram contained one interesting error. It requested arrangements be made at Arlington for "funeral services and internment [*sic*] for Commodore Kiefer."

Internment means "imprisonment or being confined, especially for military or political reasons, and typically involving large groups of people." The telegram's author certainly intended to use the word *interment*, which means "burial."

Dixie Kiefer was a man who loved the freedom of the skies, the open sea. He thrived on the camaraderie among all men under his command and disdained the typical restraints of the privileged pecking order of the formal military organization. He always pushed the limits of his independence to command his men the way he thought they should be led—not as an autocrat, but more like a father who just happened to be their skipper. A father who expected much from his men but who would do all in his power to help them succeed.

Regardless of their rank or race, Dixie insisted that all men under his command be treated with honor and respect, that their needs be met and their comfort ensured whenever possible, even if it was not always according to accepted military protocol. The "we are all in this together" attitude he exuded made his men feel that they were part of something bigger, not prisoners in an overbearing military unit. His willingness to do anything he asked his men to do was just one reason everyone who served with him loved and respected him.

Commodore Dixie would likely have had a good belly laugh over the irony in that final misuse of the word in his funeral telegram.

Epilogue

At the time this book was completed, there were many remembrances observing the seventy-fifth anniversary of the Battle of Midway in May 1942. That showdown is almost universally acknowledged to be the turning point in the war against Japan. It is a worthy thing to use such significant dates to remind new generations of historical events. Even so, it is easy to lose the human element amid the overall size and import of such an occasion—the people who were there, the ones who fought and, in many cases, were wounded or killed.

Even on the grand scale of massive war, every participant has a story to tell, and every single story, no matter how big or how mundane, helps us to better appreciate their sacrifice, bravery, and dedication. We are honored that we have had the opportunity to tell Dixie Kiefer's story—and, in the process, to have included the experiences of many more men who fought alongside him in two world wars and prepared themselves for battle throughout the years in between.

Efforts continue to have Kiefer awarded the Medal of Honor. With the passage of time, it becomes more and more difficult to gain traction toward such a goal, but it is the belief of the authors and many others that he is a perfect example of "conspicuous gallantry and intrepidity at the risk of life above and beyond the call of duty." We can hope that this book, with as complete a telling of his story as we can manage, will help that cause.

We are also committed to keeping the memory alive of all those who died for their country. This includes the six men aboard that Beechcraft Expeditor on that Armistice Day Sunday in 1945, as well as the two navy fliers who perished near the same spot almost ten years earlier.

Author David Rocco is an active founding member of the group "Friends of the Mount Beacon Eight," dedicated to that very cause. They hold regular hikes to the crash sites, participate in area events, and have placed markers to remind people that this is hallowed ground, and why. The group is also attempting to raise money to purchase a memorial for the city of Fishkill's War Memorial Plaza, as well as new markers along the trails leading to and located at the crash sites. The group maintains a Facebook page called "Friends of the Mt. Beacon Eight."

The authors salute Dr. Bill Stolfi, an avid hiker who has also been instrumental in this effort. He has organized several visits by Boy Scouts to the crash locations.

A visit to the peaceful spot on Fishkill Ridge where the Kiefer airplane went down is much easier today than it was over seventy years ago. Though still a strenuous hike, visitors no longer have to hack their way through brush as the volunteers from Quonset Point did that foggy Sunday night into Monday morning. Once visitors get there, they can still see a few remnants of Dixie Kiefer's airplane lying about. There is also a display case placed nearby with a copy of the story about the crash that appeared in the November 12, 1945, edition of the *New York Times*.

The latest figures from the Department of Veterans Affairs indicate that we lose about 300 World War II veterans a day. When we first began quoting a figure, the number was about 1,000 per day. It is so much smaller now simply because there are so few—about 600,000 total—still alive. This is one reason it is so important that we document and share their stories.

Author Don Keith maintains a website devoted to offering suggestions on how to gather and publish oral recollections to ensure that this eyewitness history does not die with those who lived it. The site is www .untoldmillions.net. He has also written articles for various publications on this subject. As of this writing, one of those articles can be accessed on the website of *American Legion Magazine* at https://www.legion.org /magazine/236273/living-history.

The authors vigorously disagree with Dixie Kiefer on one point. He told a newspaper reporter that he was not a hero.

This is not true at all. He felt he was just another working sailor, receiving adequate pay and room and board in exchange for being a full-time servant to the country he loved.

Kiefer was a bona fide hero by any definition of the word.

He and his memory deserve all the recognition they can get.

And he deserves the Medal of Honor.

Authors' Notes and Acknowledgments

Don Keith

I have written and published a number of successful nonfiction historical and biographical works in addition to novels. Because of that, it is inevitable that I am often contacted by folks who believe they have a story worthy of telling, usually that of a friend or relative, and they want to talk with me about doing it. In those cases, I almost always have to beg off. While the stories may be interesting or inspiring, they simply do not necessarily have what it takes to attract a sizable readership. These individuals would typically be better served by contributing whatever materials they have to organizations that collect oral histories and related materials, such as the Library of Congress's veterans' project.

Also, to be perfectly blunt, in order to find publishers willing to take on works nowadays, it is necessary that the publisher sees a way to sell enough books to make it worth their while. And the truth is that I also make my living writing books and have the same economic constraints. Much as I would love to do everyone's story, I simply do not have the time.

But when David Rocco dropped me an e-mail and briefly told me about Dixie Kiefer and his remarkable life, and the story of the two plane crashes on Mount Beacon, it caught my attention. It is an amazing story of a man who has not yet gotten his due. The fact that Dave had already accumulated a mass of research materials was a positive feature. And that is what led to *The Indestructible Man*. I am extremely proud to have played a part in telling Dixie's story, accurately and—we hope—compellingly.

In writing a story like this one, authors must necessarily rely on a staggering amount of research materials, such as those that David had already collected, what he has found in the interim, and what I was able to locate. We have exhaustively sought out and employed such documentation in an attempt to be as accurate as possible. In a work such as this one, almost every sentence requires some sort of backup or verification from sources believed to be reliable.

However, in the attempt to tell a human story, we have deliberately not placed footnotes or other distractions throughout the narrative, as is often done in historical works. Despite that, the reader can be confident that any statement, date, quote, or statistic is backed up with facts as accurate as we can determine them to be. We have specifically avoided speculation or embellishment, even if it might have made the story even more compelling, and even if it appeared in a source that might be assumed accurate but could not be properly confirmed.

We have also deliberately avoided a great deal of detail about ships, aircraft, and weaponry and how they work. Likewise, we have not tried to dig too deeply into military procedure, battle tactics, or excessive background information. There are many other works readily available that provide in-depth analysis of those things, including about Pearl Harbor, Coral Sea, and Midway, and aircraft carriers, carrier-based aircraft, and fleet operations.

This is Dixie's and the other crash victims' story. And we are storytellers. While we have attempted to provide enough detail to give adequate context and an understanding of what they went through, we did not want too much unnecessary information or minutiae to get in the way of the tale being told as grippingly as we could.

In addition, please understand that in our quest to make this a "human" story, we have placed words into the mouths and thoughts into the heads of people who are no longer with us. They are not here to confirm those specific words and thoughts for us. Be assured that we have based any such usage completely on our research and believe they are accurate and reflective of reality.

Understand, too, that oral histories and other personal remembrances are subject to error and faulty memories. Again, we have tried to be as certain as we could by using multiple accounts and other context, and to only use the material that we believe to be accurate.

All pictures in this book, unless otherwise credited, are from the US Navy History and Heritage Command Archives and are in the public domain. Note that some are not as sharp and clear as we would prefer, but they were taken more than seventy years ago. We have attempted to use higher-resolution scans where possible, but they are not always available.

Our research includes extensive use of the official service records of key individuals, obtained by request through the National Personnel Records Center of the National Archives. The authors appreciate the assistance of US Senator Kirsten Gillibrand of New York for assisting in expediting those requests.

We also relied on numerous newspaper accounts published at the time that reported on the crash and its aftermath. Where we quoted directly from stories, we named the specific source as part of the narrative. Note that these accounts were sometimes inaccurate or contradictory—sometimes even by the same reporter in a single story—and we attempted to confirm specifics through more than one report whenever we could.

A number of books served as source information in relation to vessels, operations, campaigns, people, and battles. Especially helpful were the books *Miracle at Midway* by Gordon W. Prange, *Blue Skies and Blood: The Battle of the Coral Sea* by Edwin P. Hoyt, *The First Team: Pacific Air Combat from Pearl Harbor to Midway* by John B. Lundstrom, and *The Battle of the Coral Sea: Combat Narratives* from the Publication Section of the Combat Intelligence Branch, Office of Naval Intelligence, US Navy. I also relied on my own previous research for my book, *The Ship That Wouldn't Die*, about another specific ship at the Battle of the Coral Sea.

By far the most helpful in this effort, though, was the tremendous encouragement and assistance from the members of the USS *Ticonderoga* Veterans Association. Their efforts throughout the years to gather and make available, through various publications and their websites, recollections from the men who were aboard the ship during the kamikaze attacks were invaluable in helping us tell what we have strived to make a full and accurate interpretation of those awful twelve hours.

The group was also very welcoming to David Rocco at its annual convention and shared graciously with him during and after that event, as well as with both Dave and I at a later convention in New Orleans after the initial publication of this book.

The authors hope we have done justice not only to their ship and shipmates, to their memories and to their service to their country, but also to all those others who have done so.

We offer this book as a salute to them, not just on Armistice Day/ Veterans Day or Memorial Day but every day that we remain free, thanks to their sacrifice.

And thank you, David, for allowing me to sail with you on this fascinating and exciting voyage.

David Rocco

Who would have guessed what life had in store for me when I left my job as a carpenter for the New York City Housing Authority in March 2001 due to a career-ending injury? An injury that set me on an uncharted course that would forever change my life. A course that I know for a fact changed the lives of a great number of other people as well.

Shortly after I retired from my eighteen-year career with New York City—one that sent me into some of the most dangerous areas of the city's five boroughs—I looked for a way to fill the void in my suddenly empty schedule.

One day in early November 2001, I came across a brochure in a rack in the Dutchess County government office building about an upstart group called Walkway Over the Hudson. This grassroots, not-for-profit, and volunteer-based organization was pursuing the crazy idea of transforming a forgotten and abandoned but historic railroad bridge across the Hudson River into a multiuse linear park in the sky. And they were looking for volunteers and donors to help them reach their goal.

I immediately signed up. This was something I could get involved with even though I was no longer physically able to do manual labor or demanding physical activity. More important, it gave me an opportunity to be a part of a single project encompassing three areas in which I had a strong interest—the perfect trifecta! They were preserving some of the forgotten railroad history in America, adding to the "Rails to Trails" effort, and it was all taking place in an area I love, along the majestic Hudson River.

The project was the restoration of a historic railroad bridge that first opened for traffic in 1889 and operated continuously until a fire burned

600 feet of the wooden walkways and railroad ties on May 8, 1974. The group's plan was to convert the bridge into a span for walkers, runners, and bicyclists, similar to other such projects in our area that had reworked old railroad beds and rights-of-way for use as pedestrian trails. This one would be considerably larger and more challenging, but that just made it more exciting for me to be a part of it.

The Poughkeepsie Railroad Bridge was 6,767 feet long and arced 212 feet above the majestic Hudson River. It had sat there from May 1974 until a group of volunteers in 1992 tried to convince the public that the walkway idea would be a better alternative than tearing the railroad bridge down and selling it for scrap.

It was six years after I got involved that the project finally took off. A local foundation generously pledged a large sum of money to get us started. Eventually, New York State Parks and then the New York State Bridge Authority assumed the operation and ownership of the former railroad span. With professional staff now in charge, volunteers like me stepped back and let them take over. We had reached our goal. Our dream was now in the hands of the people who had the wherewithal and know-how to make this project a reality. The groundbreaking was held in May 2008, and construction started soon after. The stunning walkway over the river was opened to the public on October 3, 2009.

During this time, I learned of another notable renovation effort in the Mid-Hudson Valley that sounded interesting—that of the historic Mount Beacon Fire Tower. When I became involved in the fall of 2008, the ad hoc committee members asked me to take over the project because of my Walkway Over the Hudson experience. It took the group five years to get the necessary renovations completed on the tower.

On June 22, 2013, the committee hosted a grand reopening at the base of the newly restored structure. Seventy people attended this beautiful ceremony, including three area legends—Hudson Valley master storyteller Jonathan Kruk, famed musician and composer David Amram, and my late, dear friend, musician, songwriter, and activist Pete Seeger. At the conclusion of the ceremony, Pete led the crowd in singing "Amazing Grace." What a way to cap off a great day!

While the fire tower committee and dedicated volunteers were working on the fire tower, renovations were also ongoing on the Poughkeepsie Railroad Bridge to transform it into the Walkway. When we were at the point of replacing the nine landings on the fire tower, I asked the general contractor on the Walkway project whether he would mind if I took a number of the steel walkway gratings that were being removed from the railroad bridge so I could install them on the Mount Beacon Fire Tower. He graciously agreed.

We now had the material to complete the steps and the landings on the tower, utilizing material from one Hudson Valley historic landmark on another. Both the Poughkeepsie Railroad Bridge and the Mount Beacon Fire Tower are listed on the State and National Registry for Historic Places. The tower is also included in the National Lookout Registry.

It was not long after the fire tower ceremony in June 2013 that I received an e-mail from one of our supporters asking whether I was aware that a plane had crashed on Mount Beacon a number of years before. Naturally, my curiosity got the better of me, so I started attempting to find out whether there was any truth to this story. Much to my surprise and excitement, I learned that a US Navy plane had, indeed, crashed on the northwest flank of Mount Beacon on Sunday, November 11, 1945. Unfortunately, six navy servicemen died in this crash. As my curiosity led me to research the incident more, I discovered that one of the six victims was a navy legend, Commodore Dixie Kiefer.

As part of my investigation, I reached out to a local historian and librarian, Lynn K. Lucas, at the Adriance Memorial Library, in Poughkeepsie, New York, and to Robert Murphy of the City of Beacon Historical Society, for their assistance. They were both extremely helpful in gathering important background on this tragic event.

I also learned that a group of people had come together in 2010 to commemorate the sixty-fifth anniversary of the crash with a hike to the location. Dr. Bill Stolfi of the Downstate Correctional Facility in Fishkill, New York, along with several others, had helped to organize the event, which included Boy Scouts from Dutchess County, as well as others from New Jersey and Rhode Island.

While reading about this anniversary hike, I discovered that there was still plane wreckage remaining on Mount Beacon. Shortly thereafter, I introduced myself to Dr. Stolfi and asked him whether he would be willing to work with me on a seventieth anniversary ceremony. He enthusiastically agreed.

Meanwhile, I contacted my friend from the Mount Beacon Incline Railway Society, Frank De Lorenzo, to see whether he knew the precise location of the crash. As luck would have it, he did. It was not long

Visitors at the memorial to the Mount Beacon Eight at the site of the 1945 crash. Left to right: David Rocco, James Burns, Peter Horan, and Dr. Bill Stolfi. (Photo by David Rocco)

afterward that Frank, Bill Volckmann of the Putnam County, New York, Mount Nimham Fire Tower group, and I hiked up to the crash site. It was late October 2014, a perfect, golden fall day. As I stood on that hallowed ground, I was struck with the revelation that the story of these men needed to be told.

Since the crash actually took place in the Town of Fishkill, New York, I reached out to the town supervisor, Bob LaColla, to see whether they would be interested in co-organizing the seventieth anniversary ceremony. They were. We agreed to hold the event at the Fishkill Veterans Memorial Park.

On Saturday, November 14, 2015, more than seventy people gathered to pay their respects to the six men who died on Mount Beacon on November 11, 1945. Those navy men were Dixie Kiefer, Lloyd Heinzen, Hans Kohler, Ignatius Zielinski, Clarence Hooper, and David Wood.

Also, Robert Murphy had contacted me to tell me there had been a second US Navy plane that had gone down on Mount Beacon. This accident had occurred on Saturday, September 14, 1935. In this crash, two navy reservists, Lincoln Denton and Clinton Hart, were killed. I contacted librarian Lyn Lucas, who had helped me with the 1945 crash, and she once again came through with valuable information regarding the 1935 crash and the men who died in it.

Finally, I decided to contact US Senator Kirsten Gillibrand's regional director, Susan Spear, to enlist the senator's office in helping to secure the personal records of all eight men. This effort required several months before the copies of each man's military records—at least those in the later incident—arrived at my front door in a huge, heavy box.

Dixie Kiefer's file alone took up a third of the contents in this box. It was thicker than the old New York City telephone book we once used. Shortly after that, the files of the two men from the 1935 plane crash arrived.

After several hikes and the November 2015 ceremony, some people suggested I should write a book about these men and my findings. I agreed a book should be written about the Mount Beacon Eight, but I felt this story should be put in the hands of a professional writer, to allow him or her to bring this important tale to life.

On January 5, 2017, while shopping with my dear friend, Arne Paglia, at our local BJ's Wholesale Club store, I wandered into the book department. Two books immediately caught my eye. One was called *Undersea Warrior* and the other was titled *The Ship That Wouldn't Die*. Best-selling and award-winning author Don Keith had written both books.

I looked at the author's notes to determine which book I would read first. I was quite impressed that Don had written more than thirty books, but I was more impressed and moved by the fact that he had created a website to assist people in documenting the stories of people who had served in the military or been an eyewitness to historical events. That specifically included those who had served in World War II.

Don also mentioned that if the reader had a story idea (especially one that had never been told before), they should consider getting in touch with him to discuss a potential book project.

I decided this was the opportunity I was looking for—the chance to get a seasoned author to help me tell this story. And Don was obviously an author with a great deal of experience writing about the US Navy. He had also done a number of biographies, including the life story of the famous University of Alabama football coach Paul "Bear" Bryant.

I sat down at my computer and composed an e-mail to Don to gauge his interest in co-writing a book. I deliberately did not go into a great deal of detail, giving just enough information to hopefully gain his interest.

To my surprise, Don responded within several hours. He wrote that he was interested in what I had shared with him, but he needed to know more specifics about both crashes and the people who had lost their lives. He assured me that I should not be worried about him stealing my idea since he had a reputation to maintain and uphold. I sent him the basics of the story.

Soon after, Don responded that he was very interested in doing this book with me and suggested we get started immediately. I went to work, e-mailing him all the files and documents I had on my computer and then copying every last page of each of the Mount Beacon Eight's personal records and shipping them off to Don.

It was a little over a month later when Don sent me the first chapters for my input and rewrites. I knew then and there that I had made the right decision to enlist the help of a professional writer. I was happy that I had waited for someone like Don Keith who had the skill set to best tell this story.

My initial thought had been to give equal recognition to all eight men, but the reality was that Dixie Kiefer was a larger-than-life figure. He served in the US Navy for more than thirty years and was a true and highly decorated war hero. Even so, Don and I have attempted to bring attention to the other seven members of the Mount Beacon Eight as well.

Unfortunately, as time has passed, Dixie Kiefer and the others have been mostly forgotten and remain unknown to most. I hope we have been able to show what these men contributed and the sacrifices they made on behalf of our country.

I want to thank Don for agreeing to co-write this book. It has been a fascinating journey.

There were a number of interesting and amazing things that I discovered during my research into these men and their stories. Among them:

The connection between the two planes due to the proximity of both crashes, almost directly opposite each other on the same ridge, though separated by ten years.

The connection between the Mount Beacon Fire Tower and the Mount Beacon Incline Railway during the rescue efforts in the 1935 crash.

Discovering that it was Secretary of the Navy James Forrestal who gave Dixie Kiefer the nickname "The Indestructible Man" at an awards ceremony in the spring of 1945, only for Forrestal to learn later in the year that Dixie Kiefer had perished so near the secretary's hometown.

I would like to thank a number of people who helped me in my research, assisted me in promoting various events, and made donations for a memorial headstone to be placed in the Town of Fishkill's Veterans' Memorial Park.

Big thanks to:

Bill Thomas and Mariah Hudson of Pikes Peak Library District; Michael Heinzen, a nephew of Lloyd Heinzen; and Kate Fox, a niece of Lloyd Heinzen.

Dear friends Bill and Judy Keating; opera singer and photographer extraordinaire Russ Cusick; and restaurateur Arne Paglia.

My amigos Janet, Kevin, Bobby, Tom, Whitey, Andy, Dennis Winton, Bobby Jakaitis, and Michael at AJ's at Yorktown Heights, New York; Beacon historian Robert Murphy; the legendary George Atkinson; Mount Beacon Railway Society project manager Frank DeLorenzo and president Jeff Hughes; New York State Parks Taconic regional director Linda Cooper; the Scenic Hudson organization; Rob Dyson and Diana Gurieva of the Dyson Foundation (who made the Walkway a reality); and Greg Bilotto, author of *Along the Mount Beacon Incline Railway.*

The *Poughkeepsie Journal*'s John Ferro, Alex Wagner, and Geoff Wilson; Hudson Valley News Network's Donna Reyer and Roger Connor; Cablevision's Jim Freni, Terrence Michos, and the late Walter Sands; Bruce Apar's "Bruce the Blog"; Time-Warner Cable's Michael Howard; WHUD's Sue Guzman; WCBS Newsradio 880 reporter Peter Haskell; Curtis Schmidt and Kristine Coulter of the *Beacon Free Press*; Olivia Abel and David Levine of the *Hudson Valley Magazine*; the Associated Press's Rik Stevens, George Walsh Jr., and Chris Carola; *Greensboro News and Record*'s Cindy Loman; and the *Highlands Current*'s Chip Rowe.

Fishkill town supervisor Bob LaColla; Fishkill town board members Doug McHoul and Larry Cohen; the City of Beacon's Randy Casale; Dutchess County Veterans' Affairs director Nelson Rivera; US Navy Commander Cory Barker; David Graf, Fred Vance, and Ed Trotter of the USS *Ticonderoga* Veterans Association; and USS *Yorktown* historian Mark Herber.

Librarians Lyn Lucas, Russell Franks, Catherine Dodwell, Linda Caisse, Craig Fuller, and William Thomas.

Ed Lent and Tom Masch for sizable donations to the memorial monument fund.

The Mount Beacon Fire Tower Restoration Committee.

Members of the Friends of the Mount Beacon Eight Facebook page.

Special thanks are in order for Dr. Bill Stolfi, who allowed me to get involved with the Mount Beacon Six seventieth anniversary ceremony in 2015. It was a pleasure to meet Bill and learn that we shared a common interest in the history of Mount Beacon and were both keenly interested in these two military plane crashes that occurred there. Just so you know, Bill served in the navy as well, so I also thank him for his service.

Another person whom I need to mention is Ted Davis. Ted contacted me in July 2016 to inform me that he wanted to give me Dixie Kiefer's medals and the accompanying certificates that pertained to each one. The collection included Dixie Kiefer's graduation ring from the Naval Academy.

I would also like to thank a very special person who left a lasting impression on my life. The late Pete Seeger and I became friends because of my work with the Walkway Over the Hudson and Mount Beacon Fire Tower projects. Pete was also a member of the Walkway organization

Singer and activist Pete Seeger with David Rocco. (Photo by David Rocco)

and lived on Mount Beacon. He inspired me to continue to take on new challenges to help make the Hudson Valley a better place for everyone.

I only wish Pete had lived long enough to see what Bill Stolfi, the Friends of the Mount Beacon Eight, and I have done to honor the memory of those men. Since I had many discussions about history with Pete—as well as the fact that he served in the US Army during World War II—I would have to believe that he would have given me his famous "squinty-eyed" smile and "okay" hand signal!

Finally, I would also like to thank my wife Ruby, who puts up with my projects, allowing me the freedom to do what I love.

To my father, Jerry Rocco, thank you for being the person you are, and thank you as well for serving our country during World War II. Yes, you are a true member of the Greatest Generation!

Attendees at an event on November 11, 2018, marking the seventy-third anniversary of the Dixie Kiefer plane crash. The ceremony included the unveiling of a special Mount Beacon Eight wall plaque in Fishkill, New York. Left to right: Dr. Bill Stolfi, John Deasy, David Rocco, and Larry Qualter. Deasy and Qualter served on USS *Ticonderoga* during the 1960s. (Photo by David Rocco)

And, of course, my late mother, Mary Byrne Rocco. She devoted herself to me, a child born with severe hearing loss in both ears and legally blind in one eye. She left us much too soon, but her impact on my life and on her grandchildren is a profound and enduring one.

Thanks to my children, Christopher, Jackie, and Adam, and my son-in-law, Vincent Tallarico, for all your support as well. And to my daughter-in-law, Kathryn, not only for your support but also for bringing into my life my pride and joy, my grandchildren, Cameron and Calvin.

Then, last but not least, thank you to my brother Steven, for always being there for me during all of my endeavors.

INDEX

Note: All page numbers in *italics* refer to photographs.

About the Authors

Don Keith

Award-winning and best-selling author Don Keith has published more than thirty books, fiction, nonfiction, and biography, including several bestsellers. While working as a broadcast journalist for over twenty years in Birmingham and Nashville, he won awards from the Associated Press and United Press International for news writing and reporting. He was also the first winner of Troy University's Hector Award for innovation in broadcast journalism. As an on-air broadcaster, Don was twice named *Billboard*'s "Radio Personality of the Year," and he remains the only person to receive the award twice in two different formats.

His first novel, *The Forever Season*, was named Alabama Library Association's "Fiction of the Year" award winner in 1997. He has co-written nationally best-selling military thrillers with former nuclear submarine commander George Wallace, including *Firing Point*, which was released in late 2018 as a major motion picture under the title *Hunter Killer*, starring Gerard Butler and Gary Oldman. His series of inspirational novellas, *The Last Christmas Ride*, *The Soldier's Ride*, and *A Christmas Ride: The Miracle of the Lights*, co-written with Edie Hand, has also been optioned for production as a motion picture.

Don lives in Indian Springs Village, Alabama, with his wife, Charlene. He is a sought-after public speaker, a member of the Alabama Writers' Forum, and an active supporter of local and statewide literacy efforts as well as the collection and archiving of eyewitness oral histories.

His website is www.donkeith.com.

DAVID ROCCO

David Rocco retired from an eighteen-year career with the New York Housing Authority in 2001. Since then, he has been actively involved as a volunteer for many cultural and environmental initiatives in the Hudson Valley and New York City area. He has played a major role in the successful development and eventual success of the Walkway Over the Hudson project. Additionally, Rocco has worked with the Mount Beacon Fire Tower restoration project, the Beacon Sloop Club's *Woody Guthrie* vessel, the Friends of FDR State Park group, the Yorktown Community Dog Park, the Yorktown Depot in Yorktown Heights, New York, and Westchester County's Society for the Prevention of Cruelty to Animals in Briarcliff Manor, New York.

He has been a consistent donor of whole blood for more than thirty years.

Rocco is a highly honored scenic photographer. His work has been published in many magazines and newspapers, in calendars and on various websites, and displayed in many venues.

His photos showcasing the damage and destruction of Hurricane Sandy have been on exhibit at the Arts Westchester Gallery in White Plains, New York; at the Mount Vernon, New York, city hall; and in the Museum of the City of New York.

In January 2015, he was one of the founding members of the Friends of the Mount Beacon Eight organization, working to increase public awareness of the eight US Navy veterans killed in two separate plane crashes on Mount Beacon.